The New
CHRISTMAS
TREE

The New
CHRISTMAS
TREE

24 DAZZLING TREES AND
OVER 100 HANDCRAFTED PROJECTS
FOR AN INSPIRED HOLIDAY

CARRIE BROWN

Photographs by Paige Green

ARTISAN

NEW YORK

Library of Congress Cataloging-in-Publication Data

Brown, Carrie, 1955-
The new Christmas tree : 24 dazzling trees and over 100 handcrafted projects
for an inspired holiday / Carrie Brown ; photographs by Paige Green.
    pages cm
Includes bibliographical references.
ISBN 978-1-57965-591-4
1. Christmas tree ornaments. 2. Handicraft. 3. Christmas trees. I. Title.
TT900.C4B75 2015
745.594'12—dc23   2015010993

Design by Laura Klynstra

Artisan books are available at special discounts when purchased in bulk for premiums and
sales promotions as well as for fund-raising or educational use. Special editions or book
excerpts also can be created to specification.

For details, contact the Special Sales Director at the address below,
or send an e-mail to specialmarkets@workman.com.

Published by Artisan
A division of Workman Publishing Company, Inc.
225 Varick Street
New York, NY 10014-4381
artisanbooks.com

Published simultaneously in Canada by Thomas Allen & Son, Limited

Printed in China
First printing, September 2015

1 3 5 7 9 10 8 6 4 2

To my parents, Charles and Caroline Brown, with love

CONTENTS

Christmas *is* the most wonderful time of the year, but it can also be the most stressful. The pure joy of giving is often lost in a whirlwind of obligation and overindulgence. It can be challenging to enjoy the true meaning of the holiday amid the blare of commercial excess.

But something as simple as catching a glimpse of a twinkling Christmas tree in a window has the power to remind us to pause and feel the warmth and goodwill that we love to celebrate. As a symbol of light and beauty during long winter nights, it is undeniably uplifting.

I've always thought of Christmas tree decoration as an opportunity to explore themes and ideas that resonate with me. Our homes are a reflection of us, including the traditions we choose to keep and those we create. Many of my designs spring from my childhood and incorporate elements that inspired and excited me when I was growing up. I'm forever chasing that sense of wonder; it's the essential ingredient in a spectacular tree.

Our family tree was often foraged from a farm and decorated with folk-art toys collected at home and abroad. It was a happy, multicultural riot of color that also included homemade ornaments and antique mercury-glass balls passed down from our grandparents. I thought it *perfectly* described our family. What I remember enjoying the most was feeling the presence of the tree in the house at night; it was dramatic—almost alive—and I loved it!

The first year I was married and living across the country in New York City, I didn't even know if I would have a Christmas tree. My late husband, John, who was Jewish, felt a little uncomfortable about having one, but he wanted me to feel at home. Somehow we came up with the idea of hanging a Christmas tree upside down from the very high rafters of our apartment ceiling. It was brilliant: a living chandelier festooned with lights, an un-Christmas tree for our new joint tradition.

A few years later, after moving to rural Alexander Valley in Sonoma County to revive the landmark Jimtown Store, I began to make unusual Christmas trees for the store and for clients. "Bonfire Ready" was one concept tree: a smooth red manzanita branch with lots of strong twig "fingers" that I used to impale fat

marshmallows, nothing more. I suggested to clients that they should photograph it in flames and then eat the crispy marshmallows while sipping hot chocolate. I actually sold two! Some of my trees were made from hog wire and hung with recycled tin-can ornaments, and others from the blossoms of a century plant that dried into woody tree shapes. Each season I concocted new flights of fancy.

But one particularly wet December, I just wasn't into it. Feeling melancholy while rummaging through boxes of Christmas decorations in my cold barn, I glimpsed a strand of old lights with more blue than any other color. I also noticed assorted vintage glass ornaments in shades of blue, and in a flash I decided to make an all-blue Christmas tree to express my sorrow. Then I remembered an article I had read in *National Geographic* about a blue bird that gathers all kinds of blue objects to decorate its nest. So I switched out all the lights on the strand to blue, wound it around a wire tree armature, and went in search of blue things. It didn't take me long to assemble a collection that included a ballpoint pen, a comb, a small teacup, an airmail envelope, a skein of embroidery floss, and plastic Russian toy soldiers. The treasure hunt was amusing, and I was starting to feel better.

After decorating the tree, I plugged in the lights and was struck by a jolt of blue; it was stunning and soothing. The incongruity of ad-hoc objects and shiny blue Christmas ornaments got me excited. I put the tree in the store without any mention of my thought process, and people were instantly captivated. The next day a customer asked me to make her an all-red version. Then I made an elegant everything-silver tree on a lichen-covered tree branch for our home. My blues were gone!

The trees in this book spring from the things that move me and spark a chain of free association: color, nature, food, fashion, art history, typography, folk art, self-taught crafts, and new-old concepts of *waste not, want not* recycling. I aim to make Christmas trees that are visually arresting, beautiful, and layered with meaning.

Selecting a special tree to decorate is that once-a-year opportunity to express your sense of the Christmas spirit. I hope the themes and ideas in this book inspire you to create a new look. Consider everyday objects from a different point of view; embrace a fresh color palette; include favorite elements like your children's handmade ornaments or a special family heirloom. Make something out of next to nothing with humor and whimsy that will delight your friends and family. Think of the Christmas tree form as a springboard to reinvention. Don't let commercialism bring you down—take back December by designing and making an uncommon tree!

CHOOSING THE PERFECT TREE

Just like people, live Christmas trees come in a range of sizes and shapes, whether tall and slim, short and broad, petite and perfectly proportioned, expansive, open, or slightly awkward and off-kilter. Each type can be attractive in its own way and suitable for a specific style of design.

In defense of the less-than-perfect tree, there is something to be said for selecting a tree with character. A touch of *Charlie Brown Christmas* wonkiness can add friendly warmth and appeal. Many of the trees in this book have an almost anthropomorphic look, as if they're about to walk offstage. Choosing a tree with a graceful sway or a few unsymmetrical gaps can add considerable charm and spirit.

Once you have your design concept firmly in mind, start your search for the perfect tree with a set of criteria to help you home in on the *one*. Let the hunt be a pleasure: Breathe in the delicious scent of pine, whether you're foraging in the woods, at a farm, or in a city lot.

A NOTE ON SUSTAINABILITY: Feel good about choosing a live tree! Christmas trees benefit the environment during their years of growth. They absorb carbon dioxide and other gasses and give off oxygen, helping to counteract the greenhouse effect. They provide a natural wildlife habitat, control erosion, and often thrive in poor soil that would need amendment to grow other crops. And it is common practice for farmers to plant three seedlings for every tree they cut down.

TYPES OF TREES

There are countless Christmas tree varieties to choose from, and many regional favorites. Here are some examples of trees with the general characteristics you might be looking for in your design. Feel free to substitute a comparable tree found in your area.

DOUGLAS FIR: Soft green, with medium-length needles and a lovely pine scent with a touch of vanilla. These trees grow in a natural cone shape but are often pruned several times during their growth to create an even crisper silhouette. The branches are usually very tightly spaced, so this is a good choice for a tree styled in paper decorations or ornaments that lay flat on the surface of the tree. You can substitute a **Scotch pine** or a **stone pine,** both full, conical trees with dense growth.

'SWIFT'S SILVER' WHITE FIR: Silvery blue-green, with short to medium-length needles that are deliciously citrus-scented. The branches are symmetrical, with space between to show off ornaments. Native to the Sierra Nevada, the white fir is one of my favorites. You can substitute a **silvertip,** a **balsam,** or a **Fraser fir.**

WHITE SPRUCE: Silvery green with short needles that are pleasantly balsam-scented with fruity undertones. The branches are open and delicate but sturdy enough to support heavier ornaments. Excellent needle retention makes this a good choice if you want to leave your tree up for a long time.

NOTE: Even within the same variety of tree, there can be a considerable difference in growth and shape. A denser version of the white spruce can be seen on the Galaxy Tree on page 195.

FORAGED PINE: An example of a small native tree, probably no more than two years old, with short, delicate needles. First rule of foraging: Make sure you have permission to cut. This tree was growing extremely close to an older, more established tree, so thinning it was actually a service to the grove. Chosen for its wide, triangular shape and open branches, it is sturdy enough for light to medium-weight objects.

BEFORE YOU BRING HOME A TREE

FIGURE OUT WHERE IT'S GOING TO LIVE. If you are placing the tree in a corner or against a wall, the tree will only need to have one good side, so don't worry about the back being perfect.

GRAB A TAPE MEASURE. First, measure the available space in your room to determine the maximum height and width of your tree. Remember to factor in the height of your stand or container and the tree topper. The tree doesn't need to graze the ceiling to look impressive; allow for ample room to show off its form. And remember to bring the tape measure along when choosing your tree!

THINK ABOUT HOW YOU PLAN TO GET THE TREE HOME. Some Christmas tree farms and lots offer to wrap the tree and tie it to your vehicle's roof; others do not, so call ahead or come prepared with an old blanket and rope if needed.

MAKE SURE THE CUT IS AS STRAIGHT AS POSSIBLE; this will help you position the tree upright in the stand.

TOUCH IT! If you are selecting a previously cut tree, feel the tree to be sure that the needles are firmly attached and the bark is sticky.

PROLONGING THE LIFE OF YOUR TREE

A freshly cut tree should last for two to three weeks indoors, barring excessive exposure to heat and direct sunlight. Here are a few tips for keeping your tree looking fresh.

GET IT HOME FAST! Ideally, a tree should not be out of water for more than a half hour.

TRIM THE STUMP when you bring home a freshly cut tree. Cut 3 to 4 inches off a tree that was previously cut. Put the tree in a bucket and give it a big drink of water before you put it in the stand.

NEVER LET THE TREE GO DRY. Check the water in the container every day and replenish often; trees are thirsty. (If it has been out of water for a few days, it will benefit from a fresh cut.)

POSITION THE TREE AWAY FROM HEAT SOURCES, and close nearby vents if possible.

ALTERNATIVES TO A FRESH-CUT TREE

POTTED TREES

One of the main advantages of selecting a growing tree is being able to use it after the holidays. You can plant it in your yard, or place it outside on a deck or patio and let it reprise the role of Christmas tree for several years before it outgrows its container. To use the tree inside, hide the plastic nursery pot in a larger, more attractive bucket or planter box.

DRY BRANCHES

Forage in the woods for attractive dry branches to use as tree alternatives. Take a folding saw and gloves with you to protect your hands. If you don't find one perfect branch, you can stick several in the same vessel. Pour in gravel to stabilize, and continue to adjust the branches to form a pleasant shape. Attractive bare branches are also available for purchase at floral supply shops if you aren't able to ramble around the countryside.

FAUX TREES

I'll admit, faux trees are convenient. But plastic trees don't last forever (four to five years, at the most), and—the main argument against them—*they're not recyclable*! Neither are vintage aluminum and feather trees, though with proper storage they last much longer than plastic trees. I always prefer a fragrant real tree or an arrangement of branches, either fresh or dry, but you can certainly decorate a faux tree with many of the designs in this book.

CONTAINERS & TREE STANDS

Tree stands come in many styles. Most of the old-fashioned stands have three or four pressure points or screws to lock the tree in place, and they work just fine. The stands without water reservoirs harken back to the tradition of putting up the tree on Christmas Eve. These are not suitable for live trees unless you plan to have your tree up for only a few days. Some of the newer stands have four or five prongs strung with cable wire that clamp the tree in place with a foot pedal. These stands are heavy-duty, hold more water, and secure tree trunks from 1 inch to 7 or 8 inches in diameter and up to 8 feet tall. They are significantly more expensive, but they work extremely well.

You can also turn a bucket, an urn, or another vessel into a tree stand by filling it with gravel, sand, or small rocks and water.

Here's the basic method:

1. If you will be using a fresh-cut tree, first test your improvised container to determine if it is watertight; if not, find a plastic container to slip inside. (If you are using a dried branch or an arrangement of dry branches, you won't need water.)

2. Position the tree trunk or branch in place in the empty vessel. If you want to elevate the tree in the container, pour in a few inches of gravel before adding the tree trunk. (Do not elevate the tree if you plan to heavily decorate it—you'll need the extra stability.)

3. Pour enough gravel around the trunk or branch to stabilize the tree; test it by giving it a good shake. If it's a fresh-cut tree, fill the vessel with water. Once the tree is stabilized, it's ready to decorate.

LARGE, HEAVY GLASS COOKIE JAR

ANTIQUE SALT-GLAZED CROCK

HEAVY-DUTY STAND WITH FOUR-PRONG CLAMPS

CAST-IRON STAND WITH SCREW CLAMPS AND WATER RESERVOIR

NEW GALVANIZED BUCKET

VINTAGE WOOD-GRAIN-PRINTED GALVANIZED BUCKET

VINTAGE GREEN ENAMEL BUCKET

OLD GALVANIZED BUCKET

ANTIQUE DECORATIVE TIN-LINED BRASS BUCKET

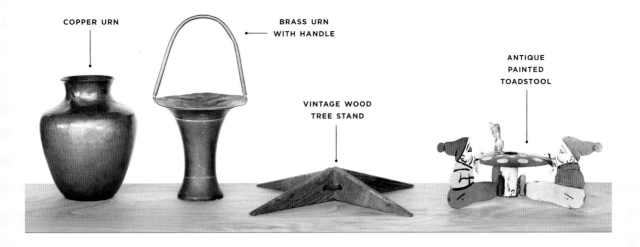

COPPER URN

BRASS URN
WITH HANDLE

VINTAGE WOOD
TREE STAND

ANTIQUE
PAINTED
TOADSTOOL

GREEN IRON STAND

ANTIQUE RED
CAST-IRON STAND

METAL RED AND
GREEN STAND

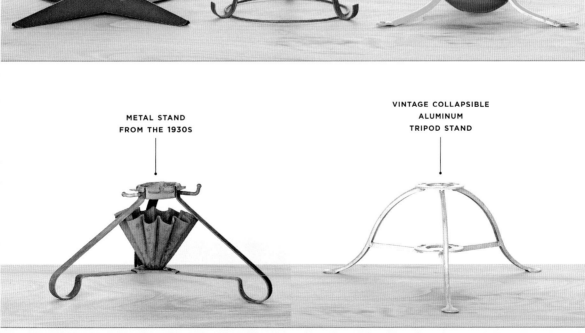

METAL STAND
FROM THE 1930S

VINTAGE COLLAPSIBLE
ALUMINUM
TRIPOD STAND

DECORATING THE TREE

DESIGN FUNDAMENTALS

START AT THE TOP. After you have positioned your tree, dress it in the following order: lights, garlands, ornaments, topper, and under-tree dressing.

CONSIDER SCALE. To make a successful, balanced composition, you must consider scale. Mentally divide the tree into horizontal thirds. Match the size of the ornament to the placement on the tree; use small objects at the top, medium-size decorations for the middle section, and larger things at the bottom. This rule of progression helps to create a dramatic sense of gravity and tension.

THINK IN TRIANGLES. Let your eye be your guide as you place objects on the tree. Every major object should have a counterweight diagonally across from it in either direction—up or down. Balance objects in trios to build strong, dynamic compositions. Scan left and right to make sure your design is bilaterally balanced as well.

BREAK THE RULES. Let these guidelines provide a good foundation for your design, but know that there are exceptions to the rules. You can add elements that are the same size in even distribution all over the tree—this flattens the composition a little but also provides a textural component that adds interest. You can also position a major piece that breaks the rules, like an object that is larger than the ornaments around it, to make a strong visual statement that reinforces the theme of the design, like the large sun on the Galaxy Tree (page 194).

READJUST. Keep moving objects and tweaking your composition until it feels just right. Stand back periodically and let your eye travel around the tree. Decorating is thoughtful work, but it's also incredibly exciting and satisfying, especially after you have gathered and crafted so many fun components to realize your dream tree design.

LIGHTS

OPTIONS

- **Tiny LED "seed" lights,** also called "LED micro-miniature Christmas lights," are available warm or cool, plug-in or battery operated, and there are even waterproof versions. They can be found at big-box stores like Home Depot as well as from online retailers.

- **Small or mini incandescent lights** can add the perfect amount of twinkle, flattering the ornaments in a supporting role.

- **2-inch incandescent bulbs** feature more prominently, generating more heat and actually warming the needles, releasing the fragrance of the fir.

QUANTITY

The current trend is to spec 100 mini lights for every vertical foot of tree, but I think that looks way too commercial. To my eye, less coverage—one third to half that amount—looks more elegant and sophisticated; but it is ultimately up to you to decide how brightly you want your tree to shine.

TO STRING

- Plug in the strands of lights before you begin, to make sure they all light up.

- Work with the lights on to better see what you're doing.

- Wind your way from the top down and around the tree in a spiral, weaving in and out to the branch tips.

- For twinkling lights deep in the tree, wind mini incandescent lights around the trunk from top to bottom. You can add another layer of lights if you desire, keeping them tucked inside and occasionally working your way out to the branch tips.

- Do your best to hide the cord ends and the connectors at the top and bottom behind the tree.

- Remember to step back periodically to look at your work from across the room. Keep adjusting the lights until you're satisfied with the distribution.

SAFETY TIPS: Don't join more than three strands of lights end to end. Plug additional strands into a power strip. Don't join more than two extension cords together; purchase longer cords instead. Turn off lights when the tree is unattended.

Position the tree with the best side facing forward.

String the lights. Divide the tree into thirds with garlands in graduated sizes.

Decorate the tree with ornaments and found objects, placing special pieces in eye-catching positions.

Wrap a complementary piece of fabric around the stand; nestle something beautiful in the folds.

TO REMOVE

Work in reverse; begin at the end, winding the lights around your arm or around a piece of cardboard. Use a piece of wire or a twist tie to keep the wound lights from tangling.

CANDLES

Little clip-on or counterweight holders for wax candles are lovely, but they are only for the vigilant. Make sure they're in plain sight, positioned away from other branches or flammable ornaments, and *never leave them lit unattended*! They also look attractive unlit and can be used solely for decorative purposes. A few styles and finishes of new and vintage clip-on holders have cups that can be rotated to adjust the candle to stand upright. Counterweight candleholders work even better to keep candles in a vertical position.

GARLANDS

Garlands create rhythm and punctuation, giving the eye a place to pause as it travels around, discovering all the objects on the tree. Here are a few styles to try.

To make a **dramatic spiral,** wind the garland around the top of your tree in tightly spaced revolutions, and then graduate to more openly spaced turns as you wind your way down and around. The distance between diagonal lines is perceived as a progression in scale and makes for pleasingly weighted proportions. To determine how long a garland you need, do a trial run using a piece of string.

Decorate the upper, middle, and lower sections of the tree in **circular garlands** in graduated sizes for maximum textural effect. Create your garlands using small objects for the top of the tree, midsized objects for the midsection, and larger objects for the lower portion of the tree. The garlands can also be made from objects that are all the same size—just be sure to space them together a little more closely at the top and gradually widen the distance between them as you work your way down the tree. I like to divide the tree into at least three tiers; you can do more if you like. To determine the length of each circular garland, use a piece of string to measure the circumference of the tree at the height where you plan to drape your garland. Add at least half again the length if you plan to drape with deep swags.

A garland doesn't have to be a continuous spiral or a full circle; it can also start and stop like **a decorative swag,** each separate length of garland dipping once or twice in a strategically placed spot on the tree. This is a particularly useful technique if you have a short, vintage garland or a strand of beads you want to include in your design.

It can also be **a single strong element** that makes a visual statement, like a big zigzag that divides the tree in thirds the way the Milky Way does on the Galaxy Tree (page 194).

ORNAMENTS

THE "PROGRESSION OF SCALE" RULE

Whether you make your own ornaments or collect them, follow the "progression of scale" rule: Hang tiny ornaments at the top, and then gradually increase the size of the objects as you position them lower on the tree. Put the most eye-catching, special ornaments in prominent places and then fill in with less important ones. It's fine to bend the scale rule by strategically placing elements slightly lower or higher than their designated-size zone if it suits your overall composition.

FOUND OBJECTS AS ORNAMENTS

Almost anything can be used as an ornament if it meshes with your theme and design. Weight is certainly a factor; carefully test the potential ornament in the desired location before tying it permanently in place—you will quickly determine whether or not a branch can support it. Some heavy objects can be nestled in toward the trunk or even tied to it.

COMPLEXITY ADDS DIMENSION

Incorporate a variety of textures and finishes; use a combination of matte and shiny surfaces, and dark- and light-value colors. If your design is built around a single, predominant color, select a wide range of hues to add richness and depth.

TO STORE

Store ornaments in clean, dust-proof boxes; wrap fragile pieces in tissue paper and layer ornaments between sheets of tissue paper or bubble wrap. Egg cartons make good nesting containers for small ornaments. Store any artwork you wish to preserve in archival boxes. Layer acid-free paper between the objects.

TOPPERS

Accentuate the top branch with a focal point—make
it something special. Angels, stars, and blown-glass
spires are traditional, but they can be interpreted
in startling new ways: Make a spiky starburst out of
unorthodox materials like needles, skewers, or candy,
or choose an object that mimics a star, like a compass
rose. You may also wish to make a slightly larger or
more elaborate version of an ornament you've created
for your themed tree.

A topper also doesn't have to be traditional; choose
a whimsical object that befits your theme, like a crown
or a nest. Other trees may be best left unadorned, as if
found in nature, or when using a bare branch that has no
definitive top point. Decide what looks best on your tree.

Once you've selected a topper, try it out on the
tree—after you string the lights and before you
decorate—to get a sense of the look and proportion. If
your topper is fragile, it's a good practice to remove it
while you finish decorating, just in case you jostle the
tree. If the topper is precariously balanced or unable to
stand firmly in place on its own, use florist or plain wire
to secure it to the branches.

UNDER-TREE DRESSING

Skip the old-fashioned tree skirt. Complement your
tree's theme by wrapping yardage of a beautiful
material like velvet or silk or a cashmere shawl around
an unattractive tree stand or container you want to
camouflage. To choose your dressing, follow the color
scheme and type of materials used on your tree. For
example, a handwoven multicolor fabric or a piece of
natural burlap would go well with a rustic design (you
might even want to paint the cloth if you're feeling
ambitious). Then simply hide the ends in back, roll
the edge under if it has a raw selvage, and adjust the
draping until it looks attractive.

Consider the space under the tree an extension of
the design; nestle objects that are heavy or don't fit on
the tree in the folds of the fabric. Decorate presents
using leftover craft materials from the tree projects.
Trees in decorative containers obviously don't need a
thing, unless you want to add a thematic object to act
as a placeholder before the presents arrive.

POPCORN, PEANUT, PRETZEL & PICKLE TREE

Roll out those lazy, hazy, crazy days of alliterative snacks and translate them into a Biergarten-themed tree for the kitchen. Who knew that glass pickle ornaments come in so many gherkin varieties? Once I started to collect them, I couldn't stop—just like eating popcorn and salted peanuts together. The 1960s Nat King Cole summertime song prompted the vision for this tree; it was an easy leap to crafting ornaments from colorful bottle caps inspired by prison folk-art chains to complete the refrain.

TREE
Foraged or purchased
tabletop pine tree with
open branches

VESSEL
Salt-glazed pickle
crock or your choice
of container, weighted
with gravel (see
"Containers & Tree
Stands," page 14)

LIGHTS
None

TOPPER
Seven-Cap Star
(page 30)

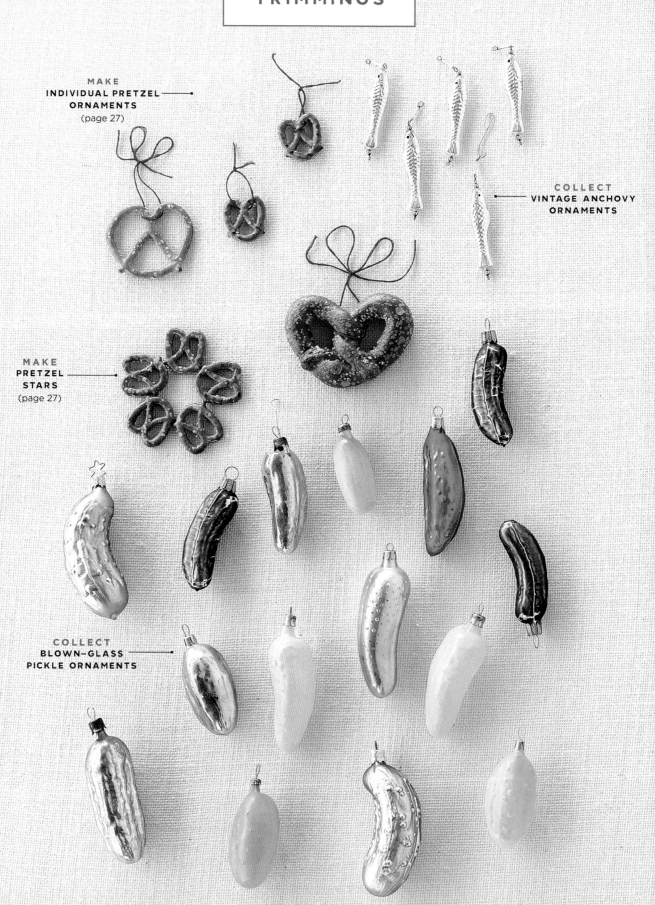

TRIMMINGS

MAKE
INDIVIDUAL PRETZEL
ORNAMENTS
(page 27)

COLLECT
VINTAGE ANCHOVY
ORNAMENTS

MAKE
PRETZEL
STARS
(page 27)

COLLECT
BLOWN-GLASS
PICKLE ORNAMENTS

MAKE
**BOTTLE-CAP
DANGLERS**
(page 28)

MAKE
**STACKED BOTTLE-CAP
DANGLERS**
(page 28)

MAKE
**THREE-CAP
DANGLERS**
(see page 30)

MAKE
**POPCORN &
PEANUT GARLANDS**
(page 26)

MAKE
**FIVE-CAP
STARS**
(page 29)

MAKE
SIX-CAP STARS
(page 29)

MAKE
**BOTTLE-CAP
RINGS**
(page 29)

MAKE
**SEVEN-CAP
STAR TOPPER**
(page 30)

COLLECT

Blown-glass pickle ornaments, new and vintage, from Germany, Poland, and Ukraine. Look for different sizes, shapes, and shades of shiny or matte green and gold cucumbers.

Vintage anchovy ornaments are optional; look on the Internet or search antique and vintage collectives that specialize in Christmas ornaments.

MAKE

POPCORN
& PEANUT
GARLANDS

WHAT YOU'LL NEED

**Large darning or
embroidery needle**

Heavy poly-cotton thread

**4 to 6 quarts plain,
unsalted popcorn**

**About 4 cups peanuts
in the shell**

Thimble (optional)

The pictured 3-foot tree features
3 Popcorn & Peanut Garlands,
in graduated sizes.

1   Thread a large needle with heavy poly-cotton thread; do not cut the strand until you are finished stringing each garland. Push the needle through the fat part of a piece of popcorn. String 6 to 8 inches of popcorn, and then push the needle through the middle of a peanut shell. Use a thimble if you find it difficult.

2   Continue to string alternating sections of popcorn and peanuts. For the garland you'll use on the top portion of the tree, alternate 6- to 8-inch sections of popcorn with a single peanut. For the lower, wider portion of the tree, create a garland with 8- to 10-inch sections of popcorn alternating with two double peanuts in the shell. When you're finished with each garland, leave a 4- to 6-inch tail of thread at each end.

3   To hang, start at the top and drape each designated size garland in swags around the tree. Tie the completed strands together or use the tails to tie the garlands onto the tree.

MAKE

PRETZEL ORNAMENTS

WHAT YOU'LL NEED

Small, medium, and large pretzels

Ornament hangers or red embroidery floss

Hot glue gun and glue sticks

The pictured 3-foot tree features 14 Individual Pretzel Ornaments and 3 Pretzel Stars.

INDIVIDUAL PRETZEL ORNAMENTS

Tie individual pretzels of all three sizes on the tree using embroidery floss, or hang with ornament hangers.

PRETZEL STARS

1. Position five small pretzels in a star configuration, salty side down.

2. Use a hot glue gun to join them together, with a bead of glue at each contact point.

3. To hang, use ornament hangers or tie them to the tree with red embroidery floss.

MAKE

BOTTLE-CAP ORNAMENTS

WHAT YOU'LL NEED

**Bottle caps in assorted colors
(you can also purchase blank
silver and gold caps used for
beer and soda making)**

Cardboard

Hammer and a small nail

20-gauge aluminum wire

Wire snips

Hot glue gun and glue sticks

Pliers

FOR THE BOTTLE-CAP RINGS:

Monofilament

Scissors

The pictured 3-foot tree features
18 Bottle-Cap Danglers,
4 Stacked Bottle-Cap Danglers,
2 Bottle-Cap Rings, and
3 Five- and Six-Cap Stars.

BOTTLE-CAP DANGLERS

Select two bottle caps and place them facedown on several layers of cardboard. Use a hammer and nail to punch a hole in each cap near the fluted edge.

2 Place the caps together, face sides out, and thread a 4-inch length of wire through the holes. Twist one end of the wire several times around itself; trim the excess with wire snips. Bend the other end of the wire to form a hook, making either a short or long dangler. Hot-glue the caps along the bottom to seal.

STACKED BOTTLE-CAP DANGLERS

Select a group of bottle caps (four or five to make a short stack, six to eight to make a tall one) and place them facedown on several layers of cardboard. Use a hammer and nail to punch a hole through the center of each cap. Thread a 4-inch length of wire through each cap to create a stack.

2 Use pliers to bend a tiny loop in the end of the wire that's at the bottom of the stacked caps to keep them in place.

3 Bend the other end of the wire in a loop for hanging.

BOTTLE-CAP RINGS

1 Select a group of bottle caps in a range of dark and light colors: twenty-eight to thirty for a small ring and thirty-five to thirty-eight for a larger ring. Place each cap facedown on a stack of cardboard, and use a hammer and nail to punch a hole through the center of each cap.

2 Thread the caps onto a 16-inch length of monofilament, all facing the same direction, alternating dark and light colors.

3 Bend the string of caps into a ring; tie the two ends of monofilament in a square knot: Loop the right-side strand over the left-side strand, then loop the original strand back over the other side strand to make a knot that consists of two interlocking loops. Pull on all four ends to tighten. Trim the ends.

4 To hang, bend a piece of wire into an S shape and slip it between the two caps at the knot.

FIVE- AND SIX-CAP STARS

1 Select five or six bottle caps and lay out your design, with each bottle cap faceup.

2 Take the cap that will appear at the top of the star, place it facedown on a stack of cardboard, and use a hammer and nail to punch a hole in it near the fluted edge.

3 Turn the caps over and hot-glue them together at the points of contact. Allow to dry.

4 To hang, thread a piece of wire through the top cap's hole, and bend it into a hook.

MAKE

SEVEN-CAP STAR TOPPER

WHAT YOU'LL NEED

7 bottle caps in assorted colors (you can also purchase blank silver and gold caps used for beer and soda making)

Hot glue gun and glue sticks

Flat wooden ice cream spoon

Utility knife

20-gauge aluminum wire

Wire snips

VARIATION: To make a Three-Cap Dangler, stack three bottle caps in a vertical row. Punch a hole in the top cap using the method described in step 2 of the Five-and Six-Cap Stars on page 29, hot glue together, and hot-glue the stick to the back of the stack.

Select seven bottle caps and lay out your design faceup. Turn them over and hot-glue all the contact points together.

2 Place a flat ice cream spoon across the three designated vertical caps. If necessary, trim it to fit with a utility knife. Hot-glue the stick to the back of the star.

3 To attach, thread a 6-inch length of wire behind the stick and twist it in the middle to secure it; wire it onto the top branch of the tree.

KITCHEN TREE

Imagine this fragrant and appetizing tree standing on a kitchen counter in a Tuscan farmhouse, festooned with medieval pomanders and gold-brushed walnuts. This is the kind of house where seasonings are ground with a mortar and pestle, pasta is rolled out by hand, and the evening *cena* is served by candlelight. Tuck a few salamis or a tin of anchovies in the branches or under the tree for extra umami flavor.

TREE
Tabletop blue spruce,
or any small tree with
strong branches

VESSEL
Enamel bucket or
galvanized pail,
weighted with gravel
(see "Containers &
Tree Stands,"
page 14)

LIGHTS
Clip-on red candles

TOPPER
Bay Laurel Star
(page 39)

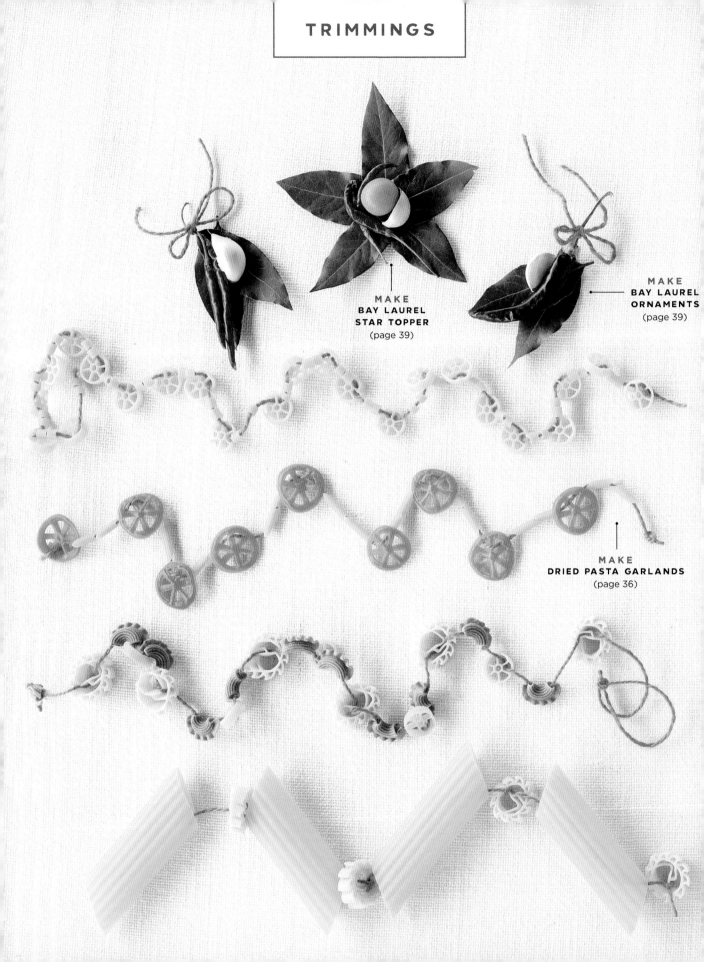

MAKE
**BAY LAUREL
STAR TOPPER**
(page 39)

MAKE
**BAY LAUREL
ORNAMENTS**
(page 39)

MAKE
DRIED PASTA GARLANDS
(page 36)

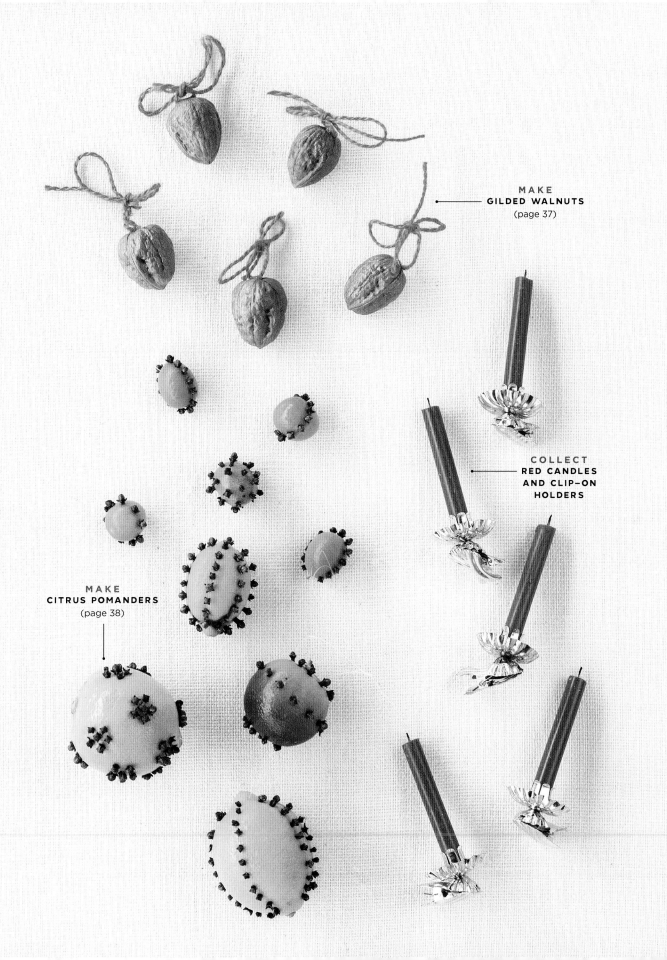

MAKE
GILDED WALNUTS
(page 37)

COLLECT
**RED CANDLES
AND CLIP-ON
HOLDERS**

MAKE
CITRUS POMANDERS
(page 38)

MAKE

DRIED PASTA GARLANDS

WHAT YOU'LL NEED

Orange jute or twine

Scissors

Clear tape

Dried pasta in a variety of sizes, colors, and shapes that can be strung, including rotelli (wagon wheels), macaroni, penne, rigatoni, manicotti, and ruffled shapes

---

The pictured 3-foot tree features 4 Dried Pasta Garlands, in graduated sizes.

1 Cut four lengths of jute: one that is long enough to generously circle the top of the tree, two to circle the middle of the tree, and one to circle the bottom of the tree. Allow extra room to drape. Wrap a piece of clear tape around one end of each length of jute to make it easier to thread it through the pasta. Tie a knot at the other end of the jute to keep the pasta from sliding off.

2 Select smaller-size pasta for the garland at the top of the tree, medium for the middle, and large for the bottom. String a few different combinations of pasta onto each length of jute, playing with alternating shapes and colors until you achieve three or four patterns you like for garlands in petite, small, medium, and large sizes. You may want to knot some of the larger-size pastas in place to keep them from slipping over adjacent shapes. Leave 4 inches of jute at both ends of the garland to tie them together on the tree.

3 To hang, start at the top and drape each designated size garland in deep swags around the tree. Tie the circular garland ends together and trim. Adjust the draping as needed.

MAKE

GILDED WALNUTS

WHAT YOU'LL NEED

Walnuts in the shell

Brush-on gilt paint

Paintbrush

White paper

Orange jute or twine

Scissors

Hot glue gun and glue sticks

Gold glitter

The pictured 3-foot tree features
10 Gilded Walnuts.

1 Lightly brush the walnut tops with gilt paint. A restrained touch looks more sophisticated than solid gold. Allow to dry.

2 Lay sheets of clean white paper on your work surface. Cut an 8-inch length of jute for each nut. Hot-glue the center of the jute to the top of the walnut, then sprinkle gold glitter on the warm glue to camouflage it. Pick up any excess glitter from the white paper on your work surface and reuse it.

3 To hang, tie each walnut onto a tree branch with a bow.

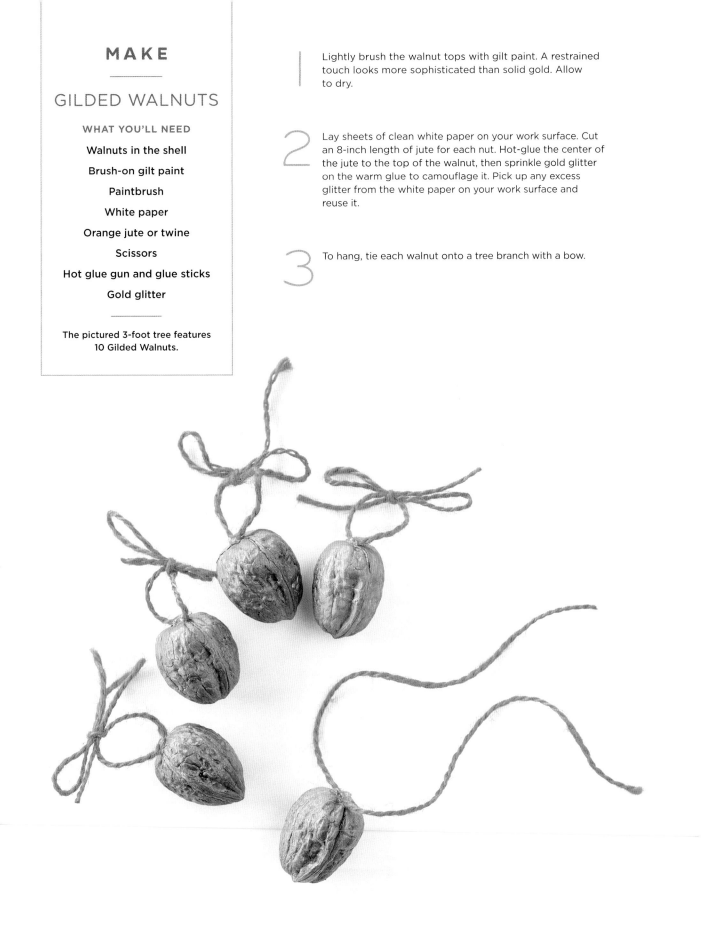

MAKE

CITRUS POMANDERS

WHAT YOU'LL NEED

Assorted citrus, including Meyer, Eureka, or other types of lemons; blood oranges; and kumquats

2½ ounces cloves

Large darning or sewing needle and thimble

Monofilament

The pictured 3-foot tree features 15 assorted Citrus Pomanders.

NOTE: Citrus pomanders that are completely covered in cloves will dry-cure, remaining fragrant and lasting for years.

 Poke cloves into the citrus, creating decorative patterns. You may be able to simply push the cloves in to the hilt with your thumb or a thimble. For thick-skinned citrus like blood oranges or Eureka lemons, you may need to use a needle to poke a hole in the fruit before you press in the clove.

2 To hang, pierce the top of the decorated citrus with a needle, thread a piece of monofilament through the hole, and tie it onto the tree.

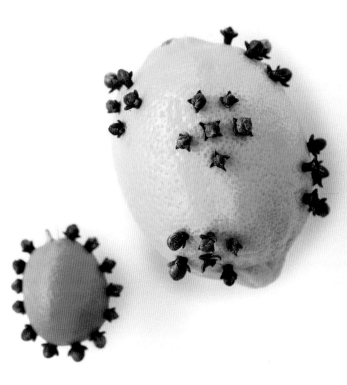

MAKE

BAY LAUREL ORNAMENTS & STAR TOPPER

WHAT YOU'LL NEED

Bay leaves, fresh or dry

Garlic cloves, unpeeled

Small, slender dried
chile peppers

Hot glue gun and glue sticks

Orange jute or twine

Scissors

1 kumquat

The pictured 3-foot tree features
7 Bay Laurel Ornaments and
1 Star Topper.

BAY LAUREL ORNAMENTS

1. Select two bay leaves, a clove of garlic, and one or two chile peppers.

2. Overlap the bay leaves at the stems, then top with the chiles and a garlic clove nested on top of the leaves. Hot-glue each piece in place.

3. To hang, cut a generous length of jute. Hot-glue the center of the jute to the back of the decoration. Tie a bow in front around the chile stem and use the two bow ends to tie the ornament to the tree. Or loop the ends around a branch and tie a knot behind it.

BAY LAUREL STAR TOPPER

1. Arrange five bay leaves in an overlapping star formation; hot-glue them together.

2. Place a kumquat in the center, nestle a clove of garlic beside it, and arrange a few chilies around the kumquat. Glue them in place.

3. To attach, cut a generous length of jute and hot-glue the center of the jute to the back of the star. Tie the star in place on the top branch.

HANSEL & GRETEL TREE

Picture a gingerbread house deconstructed, with the parts redistributed on an eye-popping children's fantasy tree. Visions of sugarplums will surely dance in their heads when they see the branches groaning under the weight of all these sugary treats, the delicious scent of pine and candy filling the air. Swoon-worthy!

TREE

White pine, or any tree
with sturdy branches

VESSEL

Cookie Jar Tree Stand
with Pink LED Lights
(page 46)

LIGHTS

Tiny white LED "seed"
lights, wound deep in
the tree and out to the
branch tips

TOPPER

Atomic Candy Star
(page 52)

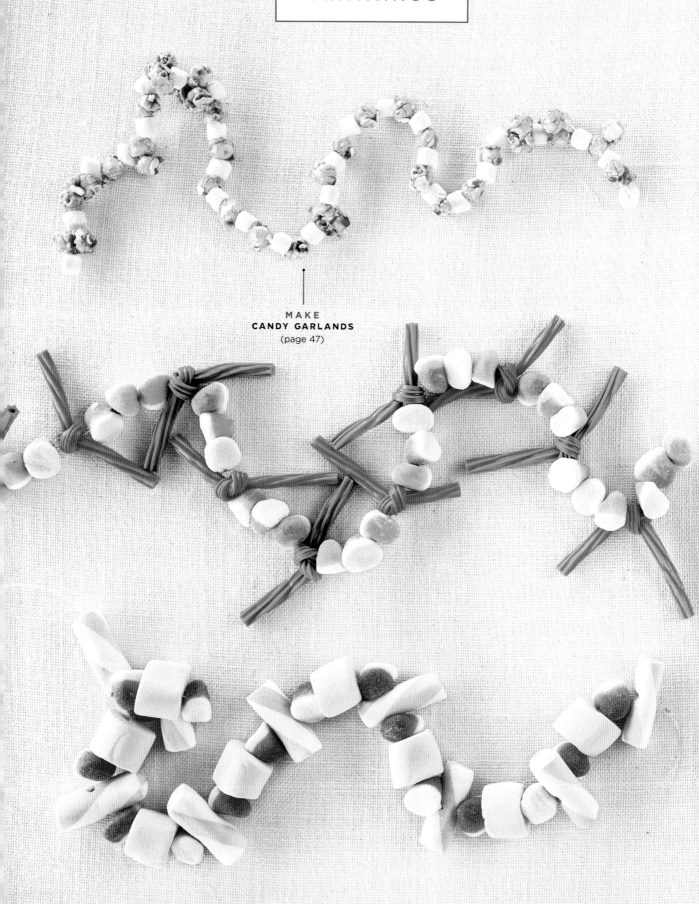

MAKE
CANDY GARLANDS
(page 47)

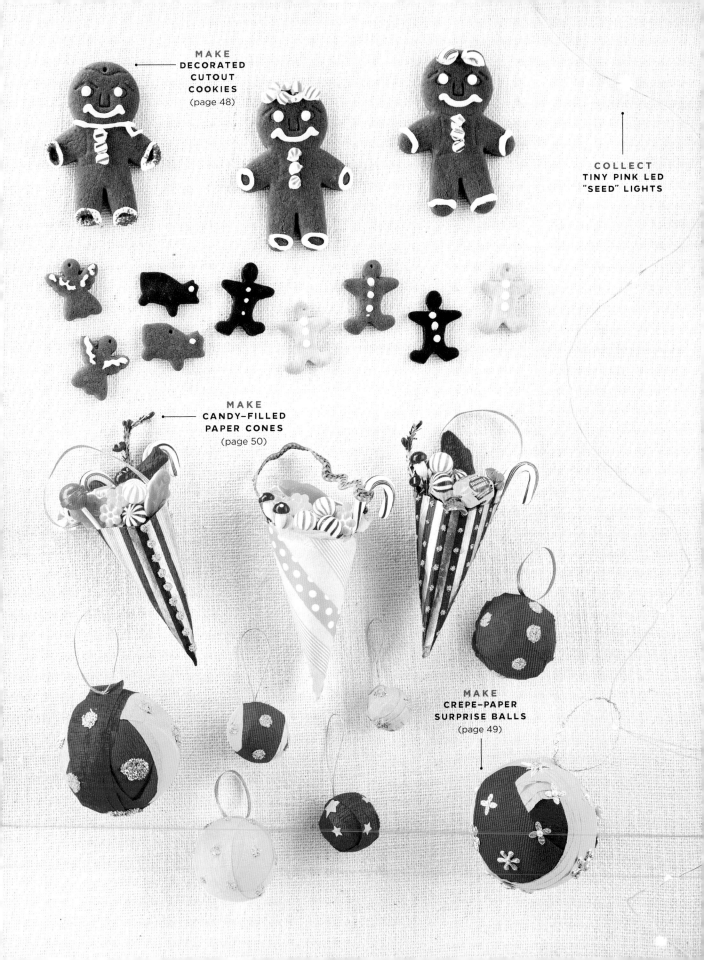

MAKE
**DECORATED
CUTOUT
COOKIES**
(page 48)

COLLECT
**TINY PINK LED
"SEED" LIGHTS**

MAKE
**CANDY-FILLED
PAPER CONES**
(page 50)

MAKE
**CREPE-PAPER
SURPRISE BALLS**
(page 49)

COOKIE JAR TREE STAND WITH PINK LED LIGHTS

WHAT YOU'LL NEED

Pruning shears

2-gallon glass cookie jar

Duct tape (optional)

Clear glass marbles (optional)

2 strands of hot-pink water-proof LED "seed" lights

1 Trim at least 8 inches of branches off the bottom of the tree trunk so that it almost touches the bottom of the jar.

2 Trim additional branches to make the tree sit level and perfectly vertical, with branches resting evenly on the rim of the jar. You may wish to stretch multiple strips of duct tape across the rim of the jar to create a web for further stabilization; leave a space in the center where the trimmed tree trunk will be inserted. You could also stabilize the trunk by filling the jar with clear glass marbles.

3 Fill the jar with water. Wrap the lights loosely around the tree trunk and insert the tree and lights into the jar; dangle the battery pack on the outside of the jar, in the back.

MAKE

CANDY GARLANDS

WHAT YOU'LL NEED

Large darning or
embroidery needle

Monofilament

Two 2-pound bags each large
and jumbo marshmallows,
in assorted colors

Poly-cotton thread

Small sewing needle

Two 1-pound bags miniature
white marshmallows

1½ pounds caramel corn

Three 12-ounce bags Twizzlers,
in assorted colors

Two 1-pound bags large
gumdrops, in assorted colors

Two 1-pound bags striped
marshmallow sticks,
in assorted colors

Scissors

The pictured 4-foot tree features
4 Candy Garlands, in graduated sizes.

> **NOTE:** The technique is similar
> for all the garland styles on this
> tree. Vary the color and candy
> combinations as you please.

1 Lay out your candy garland pattern.

2 Thread a large needle with monofilament. Sew through
the large and jumbo marshmallows, sliding them along the
line. String enough marshmallows to complete the desired
length of garland. Use thread and a smaller needle for
the garlands of miniature marshmallows and caramel corn.
For the garland using Twizzlers, tie the candy between
the marshmallows, adjusting the space between pieces
as needed. String the other candies onto the garland
using the large needle. (See the garlands on page 44
for reference.)

3 To hang, drape the garlands on the tree, adjust the
elements as needed, and tie the ends together or to the
tree branches.

MAKE

DECORATED CUTOUT COOKIES

WHAT YOU'LL NEED

**Gingerbread Cookie dough
(page 291)**

**Chocolate Roll-out Cookie
dough (page 293)**

**Roll-out Sugar Cookie dough
(page 292)**

Royal Icing (page 294)

**Cookie cutters of large and small
people, animals, and angels**

Bench scraper (optional)

Baking pan

Parchment paper (optional)

Bamboo skewer or toothpick

**Pastry bag with round tips
of several sizes (try #4 or
#5 and #7 or #8)**

**Candy canes or striped
Christmas ribbon or ball candies**

Colored sugar

Metallic thread and needle

Scissors

The pictured 4-foot tree features
3 dozen Decorated Cutout Cookies,
in a variety of styles.

NOTE: You can make the cookies
over the course of a week or
longer. Once they are decorated
and the icing is set, store small
cookies in containers with
parchment or wax paper between
the layers. Store large decorated
cookies on trays, wrapping film
across the top so it doesn't touch
the cookies. Cookies may be
stored for several weeks.

1 Cut out large and small people, animals, and angels from
the variety of doughs you have prepared; use a bench
scraper if needed to transfer them to parchment-lined or
ungreased baking pans. Pierce a hole in the top of each
cookie with a bamboo skewer or a toothpick. Bake as
directed and cool. Decorate the little cookie people with a
few dots of Royal Icing for eyes and buttons. Decorate the
large cookie people with Royal Icing; pipe features, hair,
buttons, hands, and feet. Use colored sugar and broken
shards of candy canes or Christmas candy on top of the
icing. Pipe Royal Icing eyes on little animals.

2 To hang, thread a needle with metallic thread attached to
the spool and sew it through the hole in the tops of all the
small cookies; separate a 4-inch length of thread on either
side of each cookie and cut it from the strand. Tie the ends
into a square knot or a bow and place on a branch. Hang
the small cookies near the top of the tree. Alternate cookie
colors and cluster them closely together so they don't get
lost. Space the larger cookie people around the middle and
bottom of the tree.

MAKE

CREPE-PAPER SURPRISE BALLS

WHAT YOU'LL NEED

Tissue paper

Scissors

Tiny toy prizes

Crepe-paper streamers in assorted colors

Clear-drying glue

Glitter

Glittery stickers

White paper

Metallic cord, trim, or rickrack

The pictured 4-foot tree features
15 Crepe-Paper Surprise Balls,
in multiple sizes for the top, middle,
and bottom of the tree.

Cut a few 8-inch squares of tissue paper and place the prizes in the center. Crumple the paper into a ball around the toys. You can use multiple colors of tissue paper to prolong the unwrapping experience if you choose. Wrap with additional tissue paper to make a big ball.

2   Begin wrapping crepe paper tightly around the crumpled ball, as you would a ball of string, until you reach the desired size. Tiny balls can use just one color of crepe paper. For larger balls, change colors a few times near the end of the wrapping (gluing your new streamer to the end of the previous color) to make a multicolor ball. Glue the end of the crepe-paper strip to the ball.

3   Lay clean white paper on your work surface. Decorate the surprise ball with glue and glitter or little stickers, working over the white paper when applying glitter so that you can pick up any excess and reuse it. Attach a loop of cord or decorative trim with glue to hang each ball.

MAKE

CANDY-FILLED PAPER CONES

WHAT YOU'LL NEED

Cone template (download at artisanbooks.com/newxmastree)

Computer, printer, and printer paper

Scissors

Sheets of decorative paper, letter size or larger (metallic and stripes are fun)

Washi tape (optional)

Decorative trim, braid, rickrack, or cord

Twizzlers (optional)

Hot glue gun and glue sticks (optional)

Clear-drying glue

White paper

Glitter

Tissue paper

Assorted decorative candies, wrapped or unwrapped

Mini candy canes (optional)

Spun-cotton wired trim, such as flowers and mushrooms (optional)

The pictured 4-foot tree features 9 Candy-Filled Paper Cones.

NOTE: Vary the paper, decoration, handles, and contents of the cones on your tree to make it more festive.

Print the template and cut it out. Trace it onto the back of the decorative paper.

4 Stuff the cone with tissue paper and select your candies. (If you want to give out the cones as favors, stuff them with less paper and more candy.)

50

2   Cut out the paper cone. Decorate the outside of the cone with washi tape, if desired. Cut a length of trim long enough to attach at least an inch inside the cone on both sides for a handle. (You can also use Twizzlers for handles; attach with hot glue.)

3   Use clear-drying glue to glue the paper into a cone shape; notice that the front has a little dip. Glue the edges of the handle to the inside of the cone. Lay clean white paper on your work surface and decorate the cone with glue and glitter, as you like. Pick up and reuse any excess glitter. Allow the cone to dry.

5   Fill the cone with candy; tuck in little candy canes or decorative flower or toadstool trims to embellish if you like.

6   Use a few beads of hot glue to secure the candy in place if needed.

MAKE

ATOMIC CANDY STAR TOPPER

WHAT YOU'LL NEED

One 4-inch Styrofoam ball

Crepe-paper streamers in assorted colors

Clear-drying glue

Hot glue gun and glue sticks

Assorted striped hard candies

Paper straws in 4 or 5 assorted colors, 1 package per color

10 assorted striped candy sticks

Pen, small dowel, or chopstick

10 Pixie sticks

Large gumdrops

Florist wire

Rickrack

Scissors

Wrap the Styrofoam ball with different colors of crepe paper (to change colors, glue your new streamer to the end of the previous color). Glue the end of the crepe-paper strip to the ball. Hot-glue the hard candies to the ends of the paper straws. Set aside one candy stick to use as the base for attaching the topper. Break the remaining candy sticks into varied lengths.

2 Use a pen, a small dowel, or a chopstick to create holes spaced about an inch or two apart in the Styrofoam ball. Hot-glue the Pixie sticks, candy sticks, and paper straws into the holes, alternating colors and lengths. Hot-glue the full candy stick into the bottom of the ball.

3 Hot-glue gumdrops and other hard candies to the Styrofoam ball to fill in some of the gaps. To attach, use florist wire to wrap the full candy stick at the base of the topper to the tree. Tie a rickrack bow around the topper and tree to hide the florist wire.

FOLK-ART TREE

This version of my family's Christmas tree celebrates childhood with vibrant color and whimsical crafts made with a sweet lack of pretension. Collect rustic and primitive handiwork from around the world. Or concentrate on a single country like Mexico, where the *artesania* (handicrafts) are rich in material and texture, from brightly painted tin toys, papier-mâché dolls, and pottery piggy banks to straw donkeys and miniature housewares. If you collected vintage dolls in native costume, like I did growing up, this is the perfect opportunity to display them on and under the tree.

TREE

White spruce, Douglas fir, or any full tree with strong branches

VESSEL

Tree stand wrapped in multicolored Guatemalan woven fabric

LIGHTS

Large multicolored bulbs, loosely wound in the branches and out to the tips

TOPPER

Mexican papier-mâché angel

UNDER THE TREE

Vintage and antique international dolls

MAKE
YARN DOLLS
(page 64)

MAKE
SIX-POINT TIN
STARS
(page 62)

COLLECT
MINIATURE
CLAY
POTS

COLLECT
VINTAGE
RAFFIA
GARLAND

COLLECT
PAINTED TIN
ORNAMENTS

MAKE
TIN SUNBURSTS
(page 63)

COLLECT
RAFFIA
ORNAMENTS

COLLECT
MINIATURE NATIVITY
STAR ORNAMENTS

COLLECT
PERUVIAN
BREAD-
DOUGH
ANIMALS

COLLECT
LARGE MULTICOLORED
BULB LIGHTS

COLLECT
MINIATURE
BASKETS

COLLECT
FOLK-ART
TOYS AND
ORNAMENTS

COLLECT

Multicolored Guatemalan or other ethnic **woven fabric**

Folk-art toys handcrafted from a variety of materials, including tin, wood, straw or raffia, pottery, leather, and bread dough

Vintage and antique **international dolls**

Vintage raffia garland

Folk-art topper like a papier-mâché angel or a tin star

MAKE

TIN CUTOUT ORNAMENTS

WHAT YOU'LL NEED

Sunburst and Tin Star Templates (download at artisanbooks .com/newxmastree)

Computer, printer, and printer paper

Scissors

Titanium scissors

Fat-tip marker (optional)

Nails or nail punches, in assorted sizes

Hammer

Aluminum 22-gauge wire

FOR THE SIX-POINT STARS:

Fine-tip marker

One 6-by-12-inch sheet of 32-gauge tin

Pinking shears (optional)

FOR THE TIN SUNBURSTS:

Ballpoint pen

One 12-by-36-inch roll of 36-gauge aluminum foil

Metal glue

The pictured 5-foot tree features 7 Six-Point Tin Stars and 5 Tin Sunbursts.

SIX-POINT TIN STARS

1 Print out the template for the Six-Point Tin Star and cut it out. Use a fine-tip marker to trace the design onto 32-gauge tin. Cut out the shape with titanium scissors or pinking shears.

2 Use a nail or nail punch and a hammer to create decorative patterns in the star. You can work freehand or trace circles and designs with a pen, then punch along the lines.

3 Color the tin with a fat-tip marker if desired. To hang, punch a small hole with a nail at the top of the star and insert an S-hook made from 22-gauge wire (see "Making Your Own Ornament Hangers," page 287).

1 Print all three circle templates and cut them out. Use a ballpoint pen to trace the outer and inner circles onto aluminum foil. Press firmly on the inner circles to emboss the foil. Cut the outer circle shapes with titanium scissors.

2 Cut fringe from the edge to the embossed inner circles on all three foil circles.

3 Stack the fringed sunbursts on top of one another, largest to smallest, and glue them together. Color the center of the smallest sunburst with a fat-tip marker, if desired. To hang, punch a small hole in the top of the sunburst with a nail or nail punch and a hammer, and insert an S-hook made from 22-gauge wire (see "Making Your Own Ornament Hangers," page 287).

MAKE

YARN DOLLS

WHAT YOU'LL NEED

Lightweight yarn in assorted colors: yellow, red, blue, fuchsia, orange, green, and brown

Cardboard or tag board

Scissors

FOR THE BLUE BOY YARN DOLLS:

Hot glue gun and glue sticks

Red felt, small pieces, no larger than 4 inches square

Needle and red thread

The pictured 5-foot tree features 5 Yarn Dolls, in different color combinations and styles of dress.

BLUE BOY YARN DOLLS

Cut a short length of blue yarn and set it aside. Wrap blue yarn around a 3-by-4-inch piece of cardboard thirty-six times, beginning and finishing at the same end. Tie the short length of blue yarn around the skein at the opposite end of the cardboard.

 Braid each arm and tie off the hands with short lengths of red yarn. Divide the strands of yarn below the waist belt in two, to create the legs.

2 Cut the yarn on the opposite side from this knot and remove the cardboard. Cut a short length of blue yarn and tie it around the top third of the skein to create the doll's neck; knot it in back.

3 Separate six strands of yarn on both sides of the skein for arms. Cut a short length of yellow yarn and tie it around the middle of the blue skein to create the doll's waist.

5 Wrap brown yarn around each leg multiple times to make tall boots: Tuck one end behind the leg and secure with a small spot of hot glue, wrap the boot, and secure the other end of yarn with a small spot of hot glue behind the leg. Cut a triangle out of red felt for a hat. Fold the bottom up.

6 Wrap the hat around the head, sew the points together in back, and sew it onto the doll's head. Trim all the ends to neaten.

1 Cut a short length of yellow yarn and set it aside. Wrap yellow yarn around a 3-by-4-inch piece of cardboard about twenty-four times, beginning and finishing at the same end of the cardboard. Tie the short length of yellow yarn around the skein at the opposite end of the cardboard. Cut the yarn on the opposite side from this knot and remove the cardboard.

2 Cut a short length of yellow yarn and tie it around the top third of the skein to create the doll's neck; knot it in the back. Separate six strands of yarn on both sides of the skein to use for arms. Cut a short length of yellow yarn and tie it around the middle of the skein to create the doll's waist. Braid each arm and tie off the hands with short lengths of yellow yarn.

5 Take the wrapped and tied end of the blue skein and slip it through the loop at the other end; pull it snugly to form a knot above the head (this will be the doll's head wrap). Wind red yarn around the 6-by-2-inch piece of cardboard three times and cut both ends to create a shawl. Cut two 6-inch pieces of fuchsia yarn for a belt.

3 Cut a 6-by-2-inch rectangle of cardboard. Cut a short length of blue yarn and set it aside. Wind blue yarn around the cardboard about ten times, then slip the skein off the cardboard without cutting the yarn. Wrap the piece of blue yarn four or five times around one end of the skein, about an inch in from the end, and tie it.

4 Open the yellow loop of yarn forming the doll's head with your fingers and pass the looped end of the blue skein through the opening.

6 Wrap the red yarn shawl around the doll's neck and tie it at the waist with the fuchsia yarn belt. Trim all yarn ends to neaten the doll.

7 Use a hook or another piece of yarn to hang the doll on the tree.

SCANDINAVIAN TREE

This is my contemporary take on an old-world, northern European tree starring kurbits, the traditional Swedish folk-art designs depicting stylized flowers, hearts, and animals. Originating in the seventeenth century, they were used to decorate everything from wood boxes, furniture, and window shutters to marriage contracts. Now kurbits are found as tattoos and on skateboards and couture prints. Here they hang in a Brothers Grimm fairy-tale setting with toadstools, elves, crowns, and a village in an enchanted forest.

TREE
White spruce, or any tall, lanky tree with open branches

VESSEL
Vintage painted metal toadstool stand

LIGHTS
Mini incandescent white lights wound deep in the tree; white candles in counterweight holders

TOPPER
Straw starburst

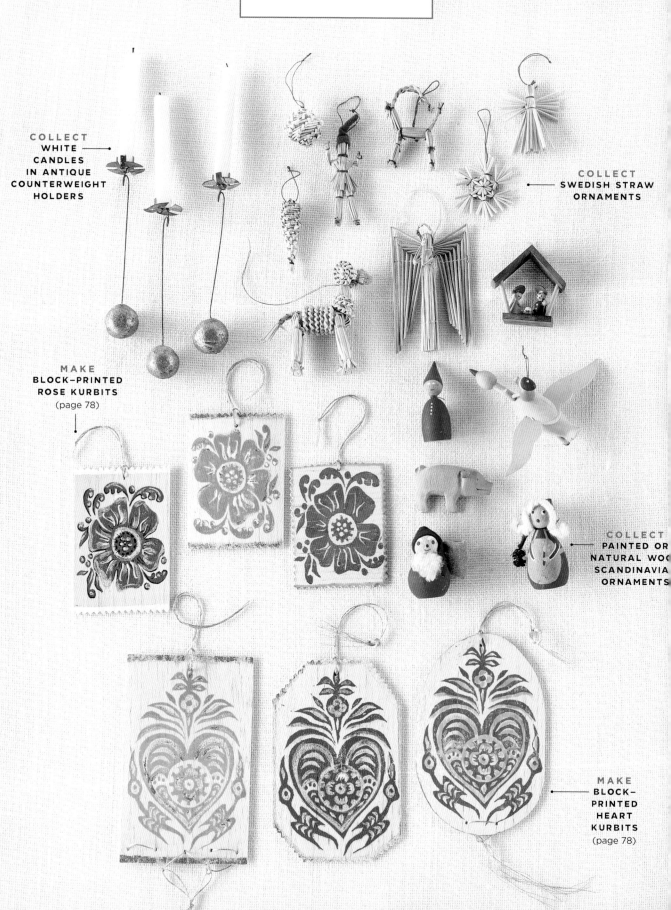

TRIMMINGS

COLLECT
WHITE
CANDLES
IN ANTIQUE
COUNTERWEIGHT
HOLDERS

COLLECT
SWEDISH STRAW
ORNAMENTS

MAKE
BLOCK–PRINTED
ROSE KURBITS
(page 78)

COLLECT
PAINTED OR
NATURAL WOO
SCANDINAVIA
ORNAMENTS

MAKE
BLOCK–
PRINTED
HEART
KURBITS
(page 78)

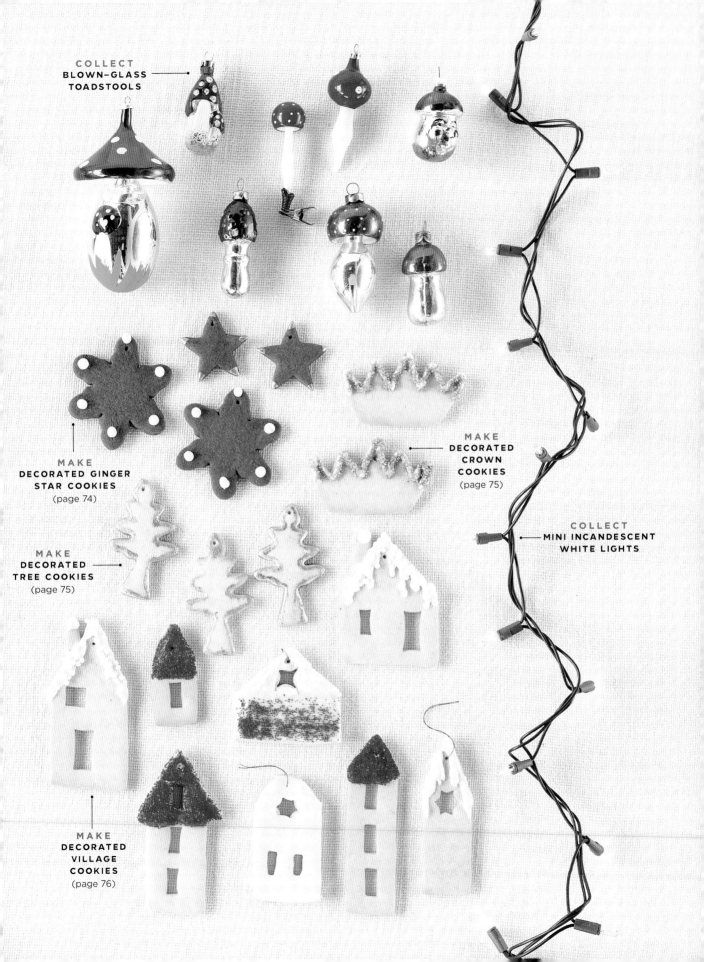

COLLECT
BLOWN-GLASS
TOADSTOOLS

MAKE
DECORATED
CROWN
COOKIES
(page 75)

MAKE
DECORATED GINGER
STAR COOKIES
(page 74)

COLLECT
MINI INCANDESCENT
WHITE LIGHTS

MAKE
DECORATED
TREE COOKIES
(page 75)

MAKE
DECORATED
VILLAGE COOKIES
(page 76)

COLLECT

Vintage folk-art tree stand; search online

Straw starburst; search online vendors of traditional Swedish straw ornaments

Vintage and new **blown-glass toadstools** in a variety of shapes and sizes

New or vintage **Swedish straw animals, angels, elves, stars, and twisted shapes**

Painted or natural wood **northern European ornaments,** including Saint Nicholas, stylized elves, animals, and nativity figures

Antique counterweight candleholders

MAKE

DECORATED GINGER STAR COOKIES

WHAT YOU'LL NEED

Gingerbread Cookie dough (page 291)

Rolling pin

2-inch star cookie cutters

Bamboo skewer or toothpick

Baking pan

Gold food-grade edible glaze

Paintbrush

Embroidery or sewing needle and red thread or gold embroidery floss

---

The pictured 6-foot tree features 6 Ginger Star Cookies.

VARIATION: If you wish, you may pipe dots of Royal Icing (page 294) on the tips of each star with a pastry bag outfitted with a #7 round tip.

1 Make the Gingerbread Cookie dough recipe as directed. Roll out the dough and cut star shapes. Pierce a hole in the top of each cookie with a bamboo skewer. Bake as directed and cool. Paint the points or edges of the stars with gold edible glaze.

2 To hang the cookies, thread a needle with red thread or gold embroidery floss and pull it through the hole.

MAKE

DECORATED TREE & CROWN COOKIES

WHAT YOU'LL NEED

Roll-out Sugar Cookie dough
(page 292)

Rolling pin

4-inch tree and crown
cookie cutters

Metal bench scraper (optional)

Bamboo skewer or toothpick

Baking pan

Small paintbrush

Embroidery or sewing needle
and red thread or gold
embroidery floss

FOR THE TREE COOKIES:

Gold food-grade edible glaze

FOR THE CROWN COOKIES:

Royal icing (page 294)

Pastry bag, 12 inches or larger,
disposable or canvas, with a
#7 or #8 round tip

Gold sparkling decorative sugar

The pictured 6-foot tree features
5 Tree Cookies and 4 Crown Cookies

TREE COOKIES

1. Prepare the Roll-out Sugar Cookie dough as directed. Cut out trees; use a bench scraper if needed to transfer them to cookie sheets. Pierce a hole in the top of each cookie with a bamboo skewer. Bake as directed in the recipe on page 292 and cool.

2. Paint the edges of the cookie trees with gold edible glaze.

3. To hang the cookies, thread a needle with red thread or gold embroidery floss and pull it through the hole.

CROWN COOKIES

1. Prepare the Roll-out Sugar Cookie dough and Royal Icing recipes as directed. Cut out crowns; use a bench scraper if needed to transfer them to cookie sheets. Pierce a hole in the top of each cookie with a bamboo skewer. Bake as directed in the recipe on page 292 and cool.

2. Use a pastry bag with a #7 or #8 round tip to pipe icing along the top of each crown. Sprinkle gold sugar on the icing before it sets.

3. To hang the cookies, thread a needle with red thread or gold embroidery floss and pull it through the hole.

MAKE

DECORATED VILLAGE COOKIES

WHAT YOU'LL NEED

Roll-out Sugar Cookie dough (page 292)

Royal Icing (page 294)

Rolling pin

Metal bench scraper

Assorted cookie cutters (optional): ¼-by-½-inch and ¾-by-1-inch rectangles, tiny four-point stars, and ¼-inch, ⅜-inch, and ½-inch squares

Bamboo skewer or toothpick

Baking pan

Pastry bag, 12 inches or larger, disposable or canvas, with a #48 flat tip (#5 round tip optional)

Red sparkling decorative sugar

Flat container, like a lid

Large white sugar pearls or coarse white sugar

Small offset spatula (optional)

Wire hangers, or embroidery or sewing needle and red thread or gold embroidery floss

---

The pictured 6-foot tree features 14 Village Cookies.

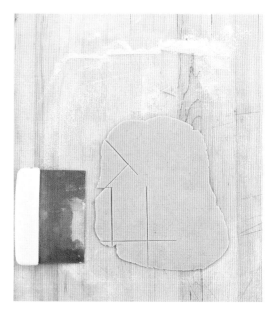

Prepare the Roll-out Sugar Cookie dough and Royal Icing recipes as directed. Roll out one-quarter to one-third of the cookie dough. Hold the bench scraper perpendicular to the work surface to make the first cuts of the house shape. Press straight down on the dough. Cut the outline of the house, carefully notching around the roof.

4 Carefully slide the bench scraper under the cookie house to transfer it to a baking pan. Make lots of different cookie building designs using the bench scraper and miniature cookie cutters. Bake and cool the cookies as directed in the recipe on page 292.

2 Continue to cut around the chimney, finishing the roof and house shape. Remove the surrounding scraps of dough, reserving them to roll again.

3 Use miniature cutters to cut windows and doors if you desire. Pierce a hole in the top of each building with a bamboo skewer for hanging.

5 Use the piping bag fitted with a wide, #48 flat tip to pipe icing along the roofline. Smooth the edges with the spatula if you desire. Spread red sugar on a flat container. Dip the frosted cookie upside down in the sugar.

6 For a snowy roof, fit the piping bag with a #5 round tip. Pipe icing in drips to form icicles. Decorate with sugar pearls or coarse white sugar. To hang, use a wire hanger or thread a needle with red thread or gold floss and pull it through the hole at the top, cut, and tie on the tree.

MAKE

BLOCK-PRINTED ROSE & HEART KURBITS

WHAT YOU'LL NEED

Kurbit templates (download at artisanbooks.com/ newxmastree)

Computer, printer, and printer paper

Linoleum blocks, 3 by 4 inches for the Rose Kurbit design and 4 by 6 inches for the Heart Kurbit design

Cotton balls

Acetone

Linoleum-carving tool set

Paint spatula or palette knife

Red and hot-pink water-based block printing ink

Glass or plastic palette, 9 by 12 inches

Brayer (rubber roller)

Paper for proofing

Burnishing tool or second brayer (you can also use the back of a spoon)

Balsa wood planks

Straightedge and utility knife

Pinking shears

Gold and white tempera or acrylic paint

Paintbrushes

Nail punch

Gold embroidery floss

Hammer

The pictured 6-foot tree features 9 kurbits.

Print the kurbit design on a laser printer.

4   Use a paint spatula to smear a dollop of ink onto the palette. Roll the brayer in a crosshatch pattern to spread the ink in an even layer. Roll the brayer lightly onto the carved block, changing direction and reapplying until the design is evenly covered. Place a sheet of paper on top of the block and use a clean brayer to rub the back of the paper, taking care not to move the paper. Peel off the paper and examine your print. If negative areas are printing, carve them away. Repeat until you're satisfied with your design.

2 Work in a well-ventilated area. Place the kurbit print facedown on a linoleum block. Transfer the design to the block by soaking a cotton ball in acetone and lightly rubbing the back of the paper to saturate. Gently peel the paper off the block, taking care not to smear the design.

3 Use linoleum-carving tools to cut away the black, or negative, areas of the design. Be careful—these tools are very sharp! Always cut away from your body and the hand that is holding the linoleum block. When you think you have carved away all of the negative design, it's time to make a proof.

5 Cut balsa wood planks to the same size as your linoleum block with a straightedge and a utility knife (cut slightly larger if you want to shape after printing). Repeat step 4, this time with the balsa wood planks instead of paper.

6 To decorate the kurbit, shape it with the utility knife or pinking shears, then paint the balsa wood edges and details of the print with gold paint or contrasting paint or ink. To hang, poke a hole with a nail punch at the top of the kurbit, then loop gold embroidery floss through the hole and knot.

THE BEES' TREE

Celebrate our endangered pollinators of sweetness and life by devoting a tree to the honeybee. Hand-felted bees buzz around an arrangement of fresh rosemary branches adorned with beeswax-dipped gold orbs and little vials of honey. The hexagonal shape of the honeycomb cell is echoed in ornaments cut from sheets of fragrant beeswax. Honor the queen bee with an antennae-sporting crown, inspired by the Byzantine mosaics in Ravenna. Buzzworthy!

TREE
Fresh rosemary branches,
or a small tabletop tree

VESSEL
Brass urn

LIGHTS
Small gold incandescent
bulbs wound in and out of
the branches

TOPPER
Beeswax Crown (page 90)

UNDER THE TREE
Jar of honey
"wearing" antennae
(see Note, page 90)

MAKE
HAND-FELTED BEES
(page 88)

MAKE
**HEXAGONAL
LAYERED
BEESWAX
PENDANTS**
(page 85)

MAKE
**TWO-DIMENSIONAL
HEXAGONAL BEESWAX
ORNAMENTS**
(page 85)

MAKE
**BEESWAX CROWN
TOPPER**
(page 90)

MAKE
BEESWAX-DIPPED
HONEY VIALS
(page 86)

COLLECT
SMALL GOLD
INCANDESCENT
BULB LIGHTS

COLLECT
ROSEMARY
BRANCHES

MAKE
BEESWAX-DIPPED
MERCURY GLASS
ORNAMENTS
(page 86)

MAKE

URN WITH ROSEMARY BRANCHES

WHAT YOU'LL NEED

Vintage brass urn with handle (or container of your choice)

Gravel or small rocks

12-inch square of 1-inch hexagonal floral or regular chicken wire (or enough to fill the container of your choice)

Wire snips

Tall (18- to 20-inch) rosemary branches or pine boughs (50 to 60, or enough to completely fill your container)

Pruning shears

Weight the bottom of the urn with gravel for stability (see "Containers & Tree Stands," page 14). Crumple the hexagonal floral wire and stuff it into the container.

Fill the container three-quarters of the way with water. Strip the bottom 3 to 4 inches of each rosemary stem (or enough to keep the water clear of any leaves). Stick some of the tallest branches upright in the center of the container, in a flat fan shape.

Continue to fill in the fan shape, with the tallest branches in the back of the arrangement. Trim shorter branches to fill in the front and on the sides.

MAKE

BEESWAX ORNAMENTS

WHAT YOU'LL NEED

Hexagon templates (download at artisanbooks.com/newxmastree)

Computer, printer, and card stock

Scissors

Straightedge and utility knife

Clear-drying glue

Gold-tone 26-gauge wire

FOR THE HEXAGONAL LAYERED BEESWAX PENDANTS:

Gold leaf

Gold hangers, purchased or handmade from gold-tone 26-gauge wire (see "Making Your Own Ornament Hangers," page 287)

FOR THE TWO-DIMENSIONAL HEXAGONAL BEESWAX ORNAMENTS:

Fine gold cord or embroidery floss

The pictured 1½-foot tree features 15 Hexagonal Layered Beeswax Pendants and 5 Two-Dimensional Hexagonal Beeswax Ornaments.

HEXAGONAL LAYERED BEESWAX PENDANTS

1 Print hexagon templates in ¾-inch, 2-inch, 2½-inch, and 3-inch diameters onto card stock and cut them out with a straightedge and a utility knife. Lightly press each paper template onto a sheet of wax and use the straightedge and the utility knife to cut around the shape. Cut hexagons in different sizes and colors to layer into a variety of contrasting combinations.

2 Dab a small amount of glue onto the back of a smaller hexagon to layer on top of a larger hexagon. Gently press the layers together. Build ornaments in combinations of two to three colors and sizes.

3 Decorate some ornaments with small amounts of gold leaf by pressing the back of the sheet onto the ornament. A light touch makes for an appealing look. To hang, pierce with gold hangers.

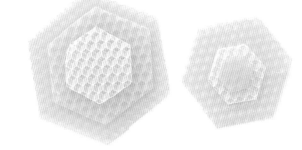

TWO-DIMENSIONAL HEXAGONAL BEESWAX ORNAMENTS

1 Print a 2-inch hexagon template onto card stock and cut it out with a straightedge and a utility knife. Lightly press the template onto a beeswax sheet and cut two hexagons of beeswax, using the straightedge and the utility knife for a precise cut. On each hexagon, make a 1-inch cut, as shown, from one of the points to the center of the piece.

2 Line up the opposing cuts and gently slip the two hexagons together until the slots meet in the middle.

3 To hang, carefully open the hexagons and wrap the intersecting pieces at the point of contact with gold cord or embroidery floss. Tie on the tree.

MAKE

BEESWAX-DIPPED HONEY VIALS AND MERCURY GLASS ORNAMENTS

WHAT YOU'LL NEED

8-ounce bar of natural beeswax

Metal bowl

Saucepan

Newspaper

FOR THE HONEY VIALS:

Plastic squeeze bottle

Tiny glass vials with cork stoppers (look for a few different sizes and shapes)

Honey

Gold-tone 26-gauge wire or fine gold cord

FOR THE MERCURY GLASS ORNAMENTS:

New or vintage gold glass ornaments in assorted sizes

Chopstick or pencil (optional)

Empty egg carton

Gold hangers, purchased or handmade from gold-tone 26-gauge wire (see "Making Your Own Ornament Hangers," page 287)

The pictured 1½-foot tree features 15 ornaments and 20 honey vials.

BEESWAX-DIPPED HONEY VIALS

 Use a squeeze bottle to fill the vials with honey. Firmly press the cork stoppers into the jars, sealing them tightly.

 Melt the bar of beeswax in a metal bowl set atop a saucepan over medium heat. (For more information, see "Melting Beeswax," below.) Lay newspaper on the counter to protect it from drips of wax. Carefully dip the tops of the honey jars in the wax several times to build up an opaque wax seal.

3 After the wax has dried, wrap gold-tone wire or fine gold cord around the vial neck and tie it on the tree. Try to position some vials in front of the lights so they glow.

MELTING BEESWAX

1 Fill a saucepan halfway with water. Use an old metal bowl for the top of your double boiler (once you use it for wax, you may not be able to completely clean it), and make sure the rim of the bowl covers the bottom "boiler" saucepan or pot to prevent steam from burning your hand.

2 Add a beeswax bar to the bowl, and melt it over medium heat.

3 Once the wax has completely melted, you can move the bowl to a counter for dipping—be sure to use pot holders! Lay newspaper on the countertop to protect it from drips. Keep the water simmering in the bottom saucepan until your project is completed.

4 Return the bowl to the simmering water if the wax becomes too thick before you finish your work. Save any leftover wax to reuse another time.

BEESWAX-DIPPED MERCURY GLASS ORNAMENTS

1 Melt a bar of beeswax in a metal bowl set atop a saucepan over medium heat. (For more information, see "Melting Beeswax," opposite.) Lay newspaper on the countertop to protect it from drips of wax.

2 Use a chopstick or a pencil as a handle or hold the top of an ornament in your hand and carefully dip the bottom into the hot wax.

3 Hold the ornament above the wax, letting it drip and cool for a minute before you dip it again to add another layer. Repeat the dipping and dripping process a few times until you build up an opaque layer of wax with a little drip bead at the bottom. (You can also dip the tops if you like after the bottoms have set.) Rest the ornaments inside an empty egg carton after dipping.

4 Hang with a gold hanger, purchased or handmade.

MAKE

HAND-FELTED BEES

WHAT YOU'LL NEED

Wool roving in shades of black, gold, white, and gray

Felting needle

26-gauge gold-tone wire

The pictured 1½-foot tree features 9 Hand-Felted Bees.

NOTE: If you have never felted before, this is a good beginner's project. But be careful—the felting needle is very sharp, with multiple tiny barbs. These barbs knot the roving together to create shape and texture by tangling and condensing the fibers. Work slowly because the tangles cannot be undone. When you make a shape you like, stop. You can always go back and felt more to refine the shape later. This craft takes practice and patience. When you master the technique, you can move on to other felting projects.

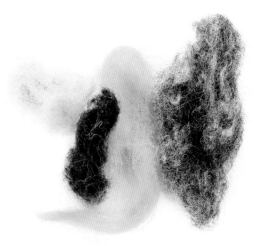

Pull off a small amount—the size of a walnut—of black, gold, and white roving. Pull off a slightly larger amount of gray roving.

4   Wrap the gray bee body in stripes of gold and black roving and jab with a felting needle to felt the stripes into place. Jab the wings into place and any additional stripes of gold or black as desired.

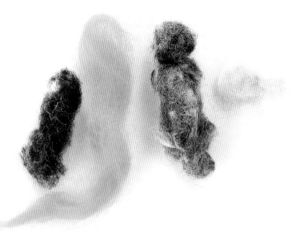

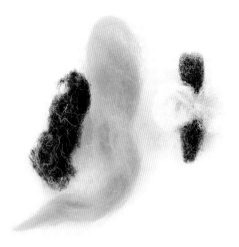

2 Pinch the gray roving into an elongated teardrop shape; this will be the bee's body. Jab it repeatedly with a felting needle to begin to create a neck area between the body and the head. Continue to jab with a felting needle, from every direction, to shape the head of the bee into a sphere and the body of the bee into its final shape.

3 Felt the white roving into a flat figure-eight shape for the wings.

5 Make two small balls of black roving and jab them into place for eyes on the bee head.

6 To hang, thread the bees onto a length of gold wire and affix them to the branches. Bend the wire as you please to create the look of bees in flight.

MAKE

BEESWAX CROWN TOPPER

WHAT YOU'LL NEED

Crown, hexagon, and rectangle templates (download at artisanbooks.com/ newxmastree)

Computer, printer, and card stock

Straightedge and utility knife

Sheets of beeswax in gold, natural, and clear

Clear-drying glue

Gold-colored leaf

Gold-tone 26-gauge wire

Wire snips

Brown, black, or striped chenille pipe cleaner

NOTE: Make extra sets of wire antennae to attach to jars of honey for gifts. Dip the lid in wax, then attach two antennae to a circle of wire, and wrap the circle around the jar lid.

Print the crown, ¾-inch hexagon, and 1½-inch rectangle templates on card stock and cut them out with a straightedge and a utility knife. Press the crown template onto gold beeswax and cut it out using the straightedge and the utility knife. Cut out 7 hexagonal "jewels" from the natural-colored wax and 10 rectangles from the clear wax.

4 To make the antenna armature, cut two pieces of wire about 10 inches long. Twist the end of the chenille pipe cleaner around the end of one of the pieces of wire, crimping the wire over the pipe cleaner to fasten it. Wrap the pipe cleaner around the crimped end a couple of times to make a little ball. Cut the pipe cleaner off, pressing the end onto the little ball.

5 Repeat with the second antenna. Twist a circle of wire to fit snugly inside the crown. You want the wire circle to be slightly larger than the crown diameter to create a little tension to help it stay in place.

2 Apply a small amount of glue to each jewel and press it into the crown. Apply a small amount of glue to each rectangle and attach the rectangles at ½-inch intervals along the base of the crown.

3 Press the gold leaf decoration directly onto to the jewels and edges of the crown; a few little touches are all you need. Gently bend the crown into a circle and use glue to join the overlapping ends.

6 Attach the antennae to the wire circle, twisting the antennae's ends around the circle several times to secure them.

7 Gently ease the antenna armature into the crown, flexing the circle as needed to work it in place near the base of the crown. Slip the crown over the top branch(es) of the tree. Bend the antennae into jaunty angles.

BIRDLAND TREE

Feather your nest with this tree sanctuary for the birds. Take a break from listening to Christmas carols with the following playlist: "Lullaby of Birdland" by Ella Fitzgerald; "Birdland," the original composition by Weather Report, a tribute to Charlie "Bird" Parker; and the evocative and hauntingly beautiful "Conference of the Birds," title track from the album of the same name by the Dave Holland Quartet. Birds congregating outside Holland's London apartment each morning, joining one another in song, inspired the bassist to write his composition, a sound poem that perfectly sets the tone for this tastefully "flocked" tree.

TREE

White pine, or any full
tree with dense branches

VESSEL

Stand wrapped with
teal blue silk

LIGHTS

White LED "seed" lights
wound deep in the
tree and out to the
branch tips

TOPPER

Bird's Nest (page 102)

UNDER THE TREE

Ostrich and emu eggs

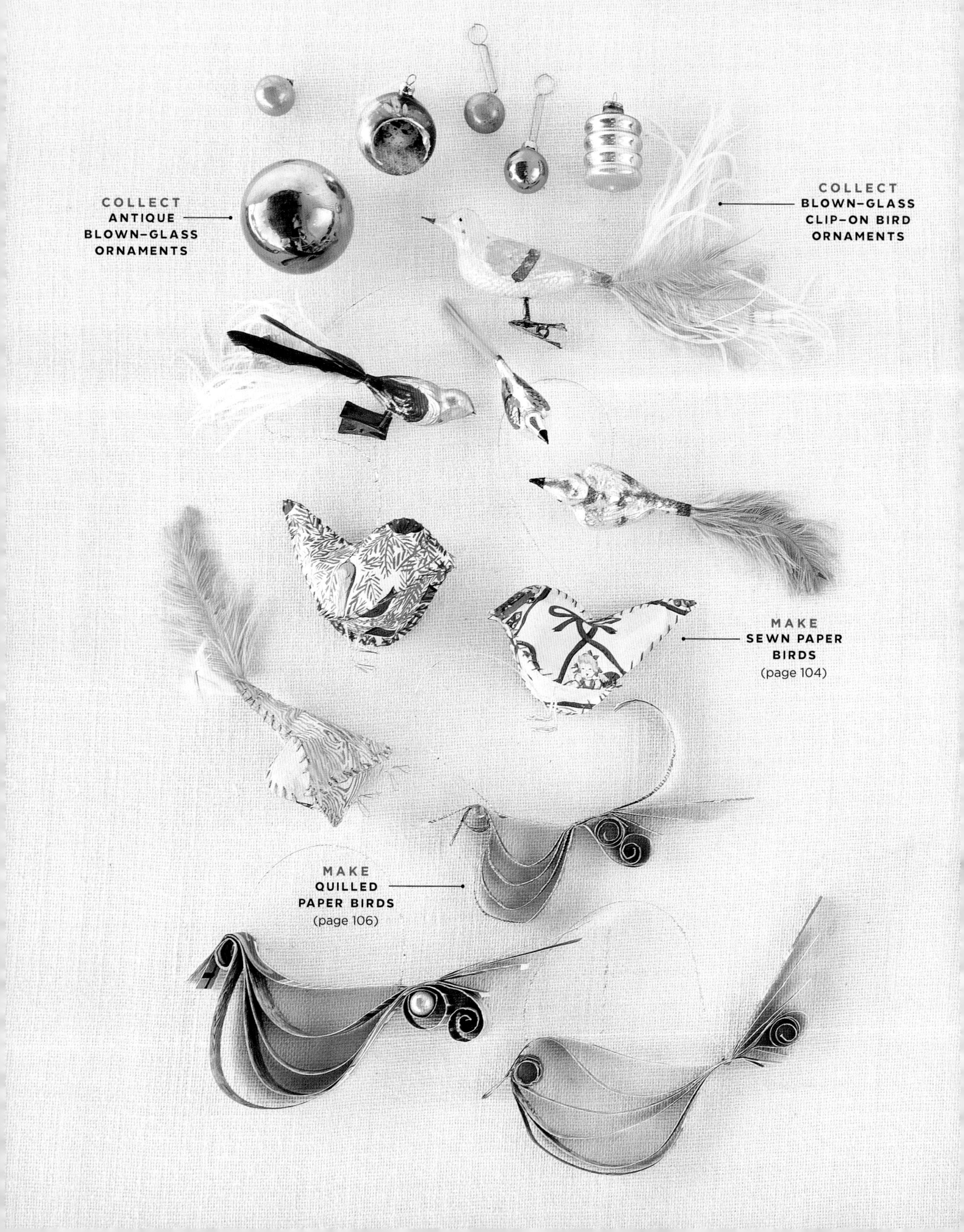

TRIMMINGS

COLLECT
ANTIQUE
BLOWN-GLASS
ORNAMENTS

COLLECT
BLOWN-GLASS
CLIP-ON BIRD
ORNAMENTS

MAKE
SEWN PAPER
BIRDS
(page 104)

MAKE
QUILLED
PAPER BIRDS
(page 106)

MAKE
PLUMED GARLAND
(page 100)

MAKE
BIRDS' NESTS
(page 102)

COLLECT
WHITE LED
"SEED" LIGHTS

MAKE
DYED QUAIL EGGS
(page 101)

COLLECT
OSTRICH EGGS

COLLECT
EMU EGGS

COLLECT

Vintage blown-glass ornaments in shades of teal, aqua, and green; look online or at antique and vintage collectibles shops

Antique or new blown-glass clip-on bird ornaments with feathered tails

Emu and ostrich eggs, found online or at a farmers' market

MAKE

PLUMED GARLAND

WHAT YOU'LL NEED

Monofilament

Scissors

1 binder clip

Large "antique" glitter in
assorted colors

Plastic container with
snap-on lid

Spray glue

Mercury glass beads

Hot glue gun and glue sticks

Feathers in assorted colors

The pictured 4-foot tree features
1 Plumed Garland.

1   Cut a garland length of monofilament. (You can make several garlands to circle and deeply drape on the tree; use a piece of string to determine how much garland to make.) Clip a binder clip to one end of the monofilament. Pour glitter into a plastic container.

2   Coat the monofilament in spray glue; coil into the plastic container filled with glitter. Put the lid on, leaving the binder clip outside of the container.

3   Shake the container to coat the monofilament in glitter. Remove the monofilament from the container.

4   String mercury glass beads onto the glittered monofilament at various intervals; hot-glue them in place.

5   Hot-glue feathers into the bead holes, and drape diagonally up and down and around the tree.

MAKE

DYED QUAIL EGGS

WHAT YOU'LL NEED

Fresh quail eggs
(2 to 3 for each small nest,
4 to 6 for each medium nest,
1 dozen for a large nest)

Medium saucepan

Liquid food coloring

White vinegar

Sheet pan lined with
a dish towel

4 to 6 small nonreactive
heatproof containers

Egg cartons, either the little
cartons the quail eggs came in
or regular-size egg cartons

Small spoon

NOTE: The eggs can sit at room temperature in the nests for several weeks—just don't drop them! In fact, I have kept dyed eggs for more than a year. Eventually the egg will evaporate inside the shell.

1 To hard-boil your eggs: Place as many eggs as can comfortably fit without overcrowding in the bottom of a medium saucepan. Cover with several inches of cold water. Bring to a boil over medium heat; *as soon as* the water comes to a boil, remove the pan from the heat. Cover the pan with a lid and let the eggs sit in the hot water for 5 to 7 minutes. Carefully remove them with a slotted spoon and transfer them to the towel-lined sheet pan.

2 Follow box directions to create teal, blue-green, and yellow-green colors. Mix ½ cup of hot water, 1 teaspoon vinegar, and 10 to 20 drops of food coloring in each container. Experiment with leaving the eggs in for shorter or longer times until the desired colors are achieved. (I sometimes start an egg in one dye bath and transfer it to another to make color variations.) You may want to leave a few eggs undyed to mix in with the shades of robin's-egg blue, teal, and vibrant green.

3 Remove the eggs with a small spoon, drain, and transfer them to egg cartons to cool and dry.

MAKE

BIRDS' NESTS

WHAT YOU'LL NEED

Leaves

Sticks, mossy twigs, and bark

Moss and lichen

Nests in assorted sizes (can be found at floral supply shops)

Hot glue gun and glue sticks

Wool roving in natural colors, a small amount of each

Dyed Quail Eggs (page 101)

Downy feathers

Galvanized or green 26-gauge floral wire (optional)

The pictured 4-foot tree features 4 small nests, 4 medium nests, and 3 large nests.

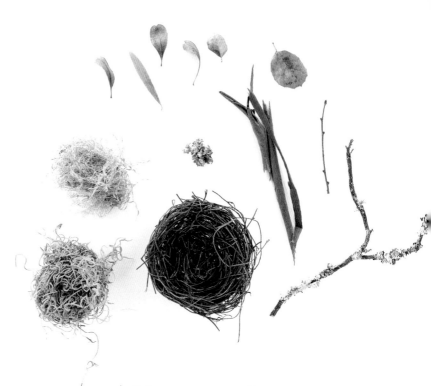

Collect an assortment of little dried leaves in different colors, sticks, mossy twigs, and pieces of bark, moss, and lichen to use to embellish your nests. Moss and lichen can also be purchased at floral supply or craft stores, as can feathers if you are unable to find them.

4 Turn the nest right-side up. Weave twigs, bark, and pieces of lichen around the top and sides of the nest; add leaves, and attach with hot glue.

5 Pull apart a small piece of wool roving, the size of a walnut, and stretch it to line the nest.

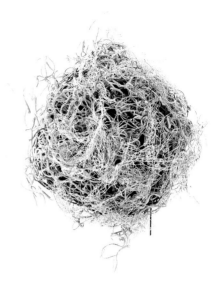

2 Gently pull the moss apart and stretch it over the bottom of a nest to completely cover. It should simply stick to the nest, but you can use a few dabs of hot glue to adhere if needed.

3 Stretch apart a few pieces of lichen to layer over the moss.

6 Fill the nest with Dyed Quail Eggs, using two or three for a small nest, four to six for a medium nest, and a dozen for a large nest. Secure in place with hot glue if desired. Add a few feathers to further decorate the nest.

7 Place the nests in the tree branches; you can also wrap a piece of 26-gauge wire around the circumference of the nest to secure it to a branch or the top of the tree. My nest topper has a small blown-glass bird in it and a larger bird perched on the rim.

MAKE

SEWN PAPER BIRDS

WHAT YOU'LL NEED

Paper bird templates
(download at artisanbooks
.com/newxmastree)

Computer, printer, and
printer paper

Scissors

Sheets of vintage or patterned
Christmas wrapping paper

Pencil

Embroidery floss, in a color
that contrasts with your
wrapping paper

Needle

Batting

Silver 18- or 19-gauge
aluminum wire

Wire snips

Round-nose pliers

Rhinestones

Clear-drying glue

Glittered monofilament
(see "Plumed Garland,"
page 100) or embroidery floss

The pictured 4-foot tree features
6 Sewn Paper Birds.

NOTE: Add tail feathers with a
dab of glue if you like.

Print the templates and cut them out. Trace them onto wrapping paper and cut them out. It's important to understand how the pieces of the bird pattern fit together before you sew them in place. You may want to make a little pencil mark on the tail so you know where to attach the breast.

4 Whipstitch the two body pieces together. Attach one side of the bird's breast to the body under the tail; continue to sew to the beak. Gently stuff batting into the bird's body; use a pencil to push it into the tail. Finish sewing the breast to the body. Use round-nose pliers to bend 6-inch lengths of wire to create legs and flat bird feet.

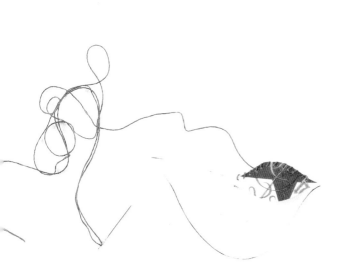

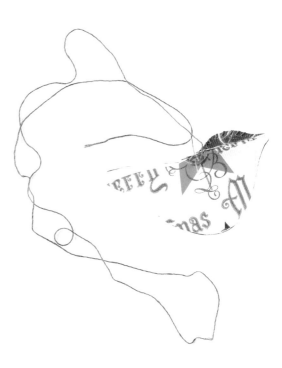

 Thread a needle with embroidery floss. Whipstitch the wrapping paper pieces together right-side out, in a continuous circle. Begin at the bird's neck and connect the top of the head to the first piece of the body.

 Join the second piece of the bird's body to the top of the head; continue to whipstitch from beak to neck.

Bend the bird's feet at the ankle, spread out the toes, and stick the bird's legs into the body. Glue rhinestones to the head to create eyes.

To hang, sew or poke glittered monofilament or embroidery floss through the bird's body and tie it to the tree.

MAKE

QUILLED PAPER BIRDS

WHAT YOU'LL NEED

Sheets of vintage or patterned Christmas wrapping paper

White glue

Pencil and straightedge

Scissors or hinged paper cutter

Wooden clothespins

Mercury glass beads

Hot glue gun and glue sticks

Large needle or small hole punch

Glittered monofilament (see "Plumed Garland," page 100) or embroidery floss

The pictured 4-foot tree features 3 Quilled Paper Birds.

Glue sheets of two different prints back to back. Let dry.

4 Glue the paper strips on top of each other at a single point about 5 inches from the left edge of the top strip; secure with a clothespin. On the opposite side of the paper strips, match up the edges of the top two strips and glue them on top of each other with a vertical stripe of glue about 2 inches from the right edge. Match up the ends of the bottom three strips, glue them together, and coil them into a circle. Glue the coil in place and secure with a clothespin.

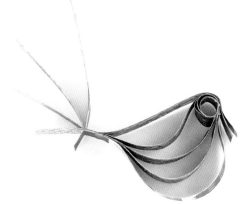

5 Glue the top two strips to the top of the coil to create a beak. Secure with a clothespin and let the bird dry. Once dry, unclip the clothespins and gently fold the strips on the left side of the bird to create tail feathers.

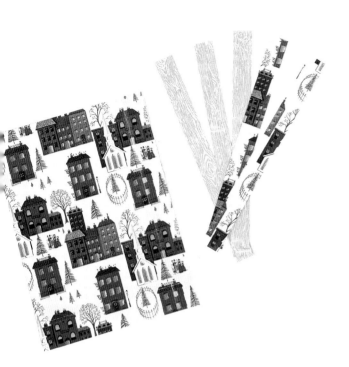

2   Cut the glued paper into six 1-by-11-inch strips (use a pencil and a straightedge to mark and cut).

3   Stack five strips on top of one another with all but the top strip facing the same direction. Stagger the stack of strips out lengthwise, 2 inches apart. Set aside the sixth strip.

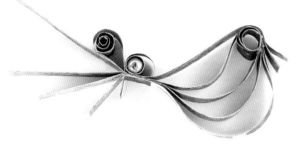

6   Coil the remaining strip as you like and glue it onto the top or bottom of the tail feathers. Hot-glue mercury glass beads in the center of the additional coil or into the eye coil.

7   To hang, make a hole with a large needle or a small hole punch on the top of the bird and use glittered monofilament or embroidery floss to tie the bird to the tree.

WOODLAND TREE

A fanciful habitat for sylvan elves rises from an old stump, as if discovered in a clearing deep in the woods. It's a tree that St. Francis of Assisi might approve of, paying tribute to bird lovers and humble foragers. Fragrant Madonna lilies, depicted in Annunciation paintings dating from the Middle Ages, are loosely tucked about, and candles flicker. It all feels a little windblown and magical.

Think of this tree as a living floral arrangement, ideal for a dinner party or the night before Christmas Eve. It's ephemeral, lasting four to five days—or longer if you put the tree in water instead of a stump.

TREE
Foraged pine, or any
tree with loose and
open branches

VESSEL
Moss-Covered Tree
Stump (page 112)

LIGHTS
Small white lights
wound around
the trunk and out
onto the branches;
white candles in
counterweight holders

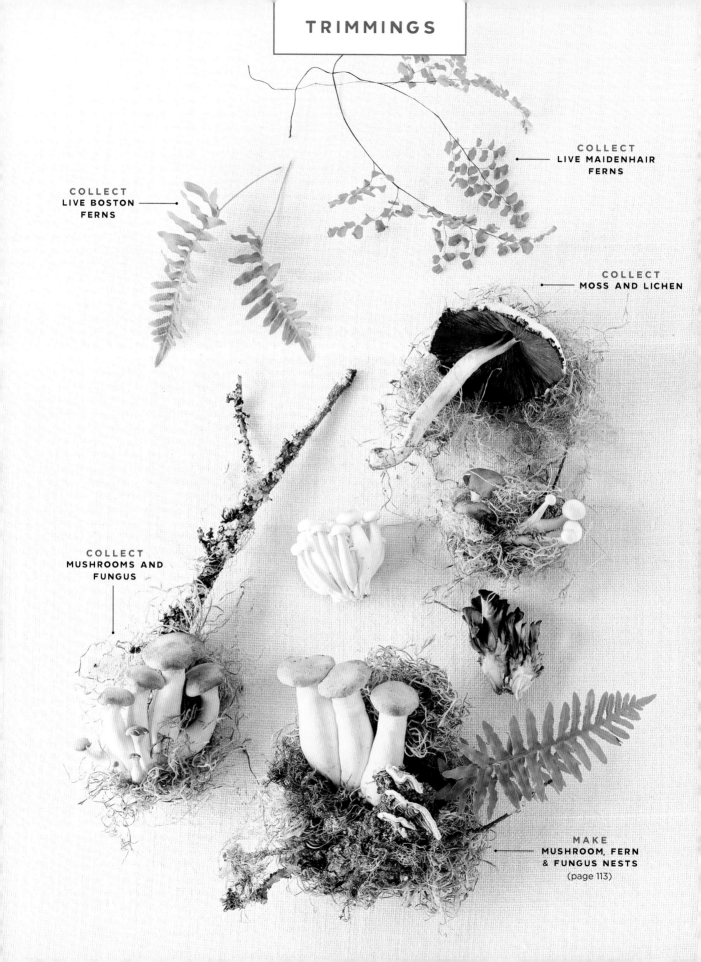

TRIMMINGS

COLLECT
LIVE MAIDENHAIR
FERNS

COLLECT
LIVE BOSTON
FERNS

COLLECT
MOSS AND LICHEN

COLLECT
MUSHROOMS AND
FUNGUS

MAKE
MUSHROOM, FERN
& FUNGUS NESTS
(page 113)

MAKE
BIRDSEED-
ENCRUSTED
PAPER LEAVES
(page 114)

COLLECT
WHITE
CANDLES IN
COUNTERWEIGHT
HOLDERS

MAKE
BIRDSEED-
ENCRUSTED
PINECONES
(page 114)

COLLECT
SMALL WHITE
LIGHTS

COLLECT
TWIGS AND
STICKS

COLLECT
WHITE
MADONNA
LILIES

MAKE

MOSS-COVERED TREE STUMP

WHAT YOU'LL NEED

Tree stump

Drill with large (1- to 1½-inch)
bit or spade drill bit

Wine corks (optional)

Hot glue gun and glue sticks

Moss

NOTE: If you wish, you can add
a toadstool or two to the side of
the stump. Attach a little tuft of
moss to hide the glue.

1 Drill a 3-inch-deep hole, approximately the diameter of
your tree trunk, in the top of a stump. If necessary, drill
multiple holes close together to enlarge the diameter of the
hole to accommodate the tree trunk. You may want to use
a spade bit if the wood is hard. Drill a pilot hole to mark the
center first for extra security so the spade bit doesn't drift.
It doesn't matter if the hole isn't perfectly round. You can
use sliced pieces of wine corks to shim the tree in place.

2 Hot-glue moss around the tree trunk.

MAKE

MUSHROOM, FERN & FUNGUS NESTS

WHAT YOU'LL NEED

1 to 2 quarts of sphagnum moss (available at floral supply stores; look for fresh, bright green moss)

Lichen

Fresh mushrooms in different sizes and shapes, such as oyster, straw, Enoki, shiitake, hen-of-the-woods, and even foraged toadstools

Fern fronds

22-gauge floral wire

Wire snips

Hot glue gun and glue sticks (optional)

3- or 4-inch water vials or floral tubes (optional)

Foraged tree fungus (optional; look for bracken on dead logs and branches; break off chunks with some moss attached if possible)

Foraged stick with lichen (optional)

The pictured 5-foot tree features 7 Mushroom, Fern & Fungus Nests.

1 Make a little nest out of the moss and lichen.

2 Tuck the mushrooms and ferns into the nest and wrap floral wire around the nest several times to bind everything together. Use a dab of hot glue at the base of the mushrooms if you have difficulty keeping the nest intact. You can also slip the ferns into a small water vial to keep them fresh, then sink the vial into the nest. You may choose to decorate the nest with a little tree fungus after you wire it together.

3 To hang, wrap the wire around a branch or the tree trunk to secure in place. You can use additional wire to attach the nest to a lichen-covered stick to help prop up the nest in the desired position. Once the nest is secure, you can stick in additional large mushrooms with slender stems.

MAKE

BIRDSEED-ENCRUSTED PINECONES & PAPER LEAVES

WHAT YOU'LL NEED

Newspaper

Wheat paste (page 294)

Small stiff-bristle paintbrush

Blend of birdseed mix

FOR THE PINECONES:

Pinecones in different sizes

Flat-backed
rhinestones (optional)

Monofilament or green floral wire

FOR THE PAPER LEAVES:

Leaf templates (download
at artisanbooks.com/
newxmastree)

Computer, printer, and
card stock

Utility knife

Rotary stitch marker (optional)

Needle

Green ornament hangers or
green floral wire

The pictured 5-foot tree features
17 pinecones and 12 paper leaves.

NOTE: Hang these seed-crusted
pinecones and leaves outside for
the birds to enjoy after Christmas.
Even the paste is edible.

BIRDSEED-ENCRUSTED PINECONES

1 Lay newspaper on your work surface. Dab the wheat paste on the base of the pinecone with a stiff-bristle brush, applying it between the bracts.

2 Sprinkle birdseed over the paste, being sure to work over the newspaper to catch the seed to reuse. Continue to apply the birdseed until you have completely covered the paste. Dry the encrusted pinecone overnight. If you'd like to add rhinestones to the top of the pinecone, adhere them with a dab of paste.

3 To hang, work a length of monofilament or green wire in between the bracts at the base of the pinecone. Twist the wire or knot the monofilament, and tie on the tree.

BIRDSEED-ENCRUSTED PAPER LEAVES

1 Print the template on card stock and cut it out with a utility knife. To give the leaf extra dimension, you can use a rotary stitch marker to create a curving line from stem to tip and gently bend along the line.

2 Lay newspaper on your work surface. Paint the leaf with paste (you may coat the entire leaf front, or just one half) and sprinkle with birdseed to cover; reuse any seed that falls onto the newspaper.

3 To hang, poke a hole in the stem with a needle, thread the hanger or a piece of floral wire through it, and bend. These look particularly good on the outer tips of the branches.

LILIES & FERNS

WHAT YOU'LL NEED

12 White Madonna lily stems, with open and closed flowers

Assorted small ferns: maidenhair, Boston, and beech (either purchased or foraged)

3- or 4-inch-long water vials or floral tubes

Green floral wire

Moss- or lichen-covered sticks (optional)

The pictured 5-foot tree features 12 lilies and 12 ferns.

NOTE: Mist the ferns daily to keep them looking fresh and happy.

1   Tuck several lily stems cut on an angle or sprigs of fern into capped, water-filled vials.

2   To hang, wrap a generous length of floral wire around the cap of each vial and use the wire to secure the vial to a branch. Hide the vial deep in the tree, behind one of the mossy nests or along the top of a branch; you can also camouflage the vials with clusters of moss- or lichen-covered sticks. The water vials may leak a little, so check and refill as needed.

1 Cluster denser groupings of lilies, ferns, and large pinecones on the lower branches of the tree. If the branches sag too much under the weight of the large pinecones, lift by tying a strand of monofilament or wire midbranch and secure the other end to the trunk.

2 Position mushroom, fern, and fungus nests and lilies in the middle and upper branches of the tree.

3 After arranging and layering the major components to your satisfaction, weave in lichen-covered sticks and drifts of moss to further blend the decorations into the tree and camouflage the wires and vials.

4 Hang smaller birdseed- and moss-covered pinecones on the inner and outer branches of the tree, top to bottom. Hang birdseed-encrusted leaves on the outer branch tips, top to bottom.

SILVER TREE

Elegant and delicate, this silvery, soft-spoken tree of bare branches looks sublime in winter light. Combine unexpected found objects and vintage Christmas ornaments in all finishes of silver, the more tarnished the patina the better. This is a grown-up, sophisticated tree: a touch of Miss Havisham with a sly sense of humor.

TREE

Manzanita branch with
a few remaining leaves,
or any purchased or
foraged bare branch

VESSEL

Vintage wood tree stand
with stretchy metal coil
threaded through each
of the four feet, draped
in light gray cashmere
shawl (page 124)

LIGHTS

White candles in silver
clip-on holders

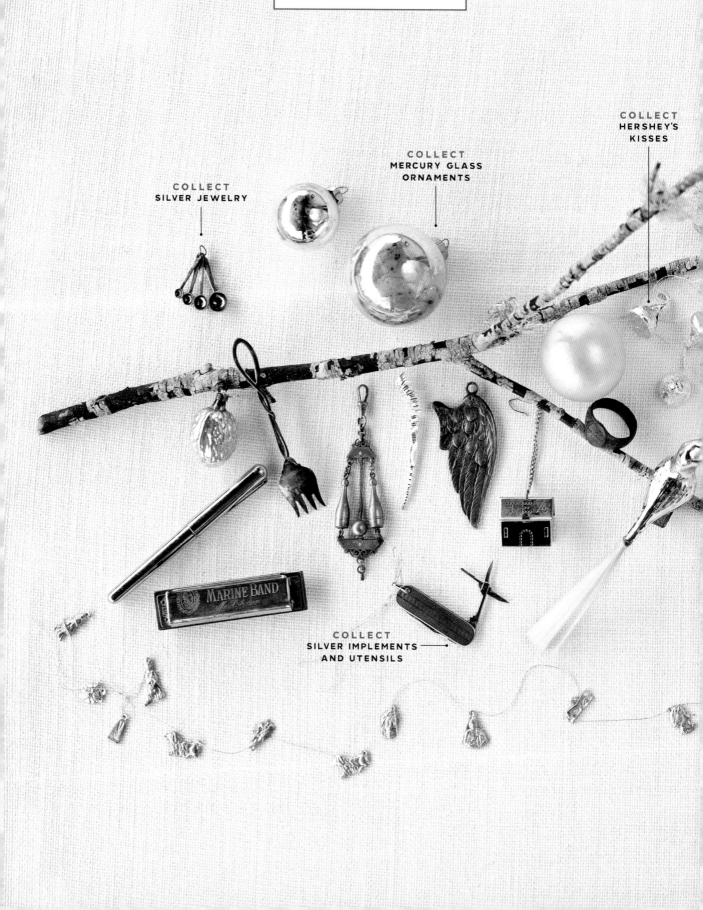

TRIMMINGS

COLLECT
HERSHEY'S
KISSES

COLLECT
MERCURY GLASS
ORNAMENTS

COLLECT
SILVER JEWELRY

COLLECT
SILVER IMPLEMENTS
AND UTENSILS

MARINE BAND

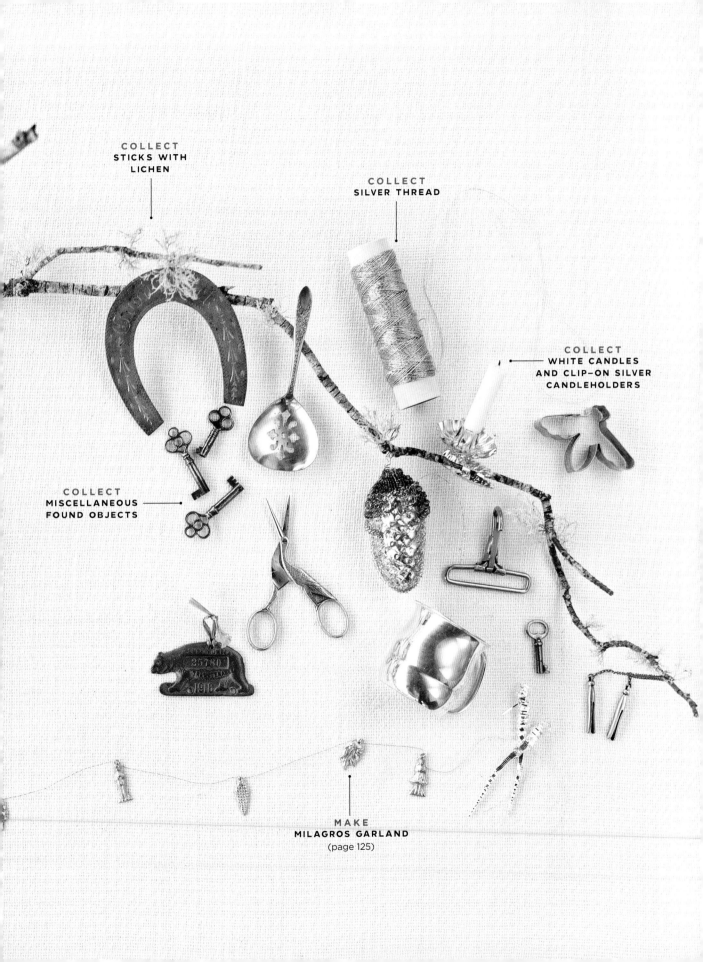

COLLECT
STICKS WITH
LICHEN

COLLECT
SILVER THREAD

COLLECT
WHITE CANDLES
AND CLIP-ON SILVER
CANDLEHOLDERS

COLLECT
MISCELLANEOUS
FOUND OBJECTS

MAKE
MILAGROS GARLAND
(page 125)

COLLECT

Antique or new silver **mercury glass ornaments** in various shapes and sizes, matte and shiny

Sterling or silver-plate and pewter **implements and utensils**

Silver **jewelry,** including bracelets, charms, or milagros

Silver **thread, cord, raffia, or satin ribbon**

Random silvery items like pens, keys, buckles, dog chains, a protractor

Hershey's Kisses

Foraged sticks with lichen and delicate moss

MAKE

DRY BRANCH
TREE IN STAND

WHAT YOU'LL NEED

Tree stand

Manzanita branch

Several large rocks

**Gray cashmere shawl or other
silvery-gray fabric**

1   Insert the branch into a vintage wood stand with a stretchy
coil that holds the branch in place, or any stand with feet.

2   Arrange rocks to weight the stand on all sides.

3   Drape the rocks and stand with fabric; play with the
folds until it looks attractive, like the drapery in an old still-
life painting.

MAKE

MILAGROS GARLAND

WHAT YOU'LL NEED

Silver cord or embroidery floss

Scissors

28 to 30 silver cast-metal milagros

The pictured 5-foot tree features 1 Milagros Garland.

NOTE: You can use antique or old keys instead of milagros, tie Hershey's Kisses onto a stretch of garland, or even make a simple paper-clip chain.

Cut a length of silver cord long enough to drape around your tree. Knot milagros at evenly spaced intervals, 3 to 4 inches apart, along the length of cord.

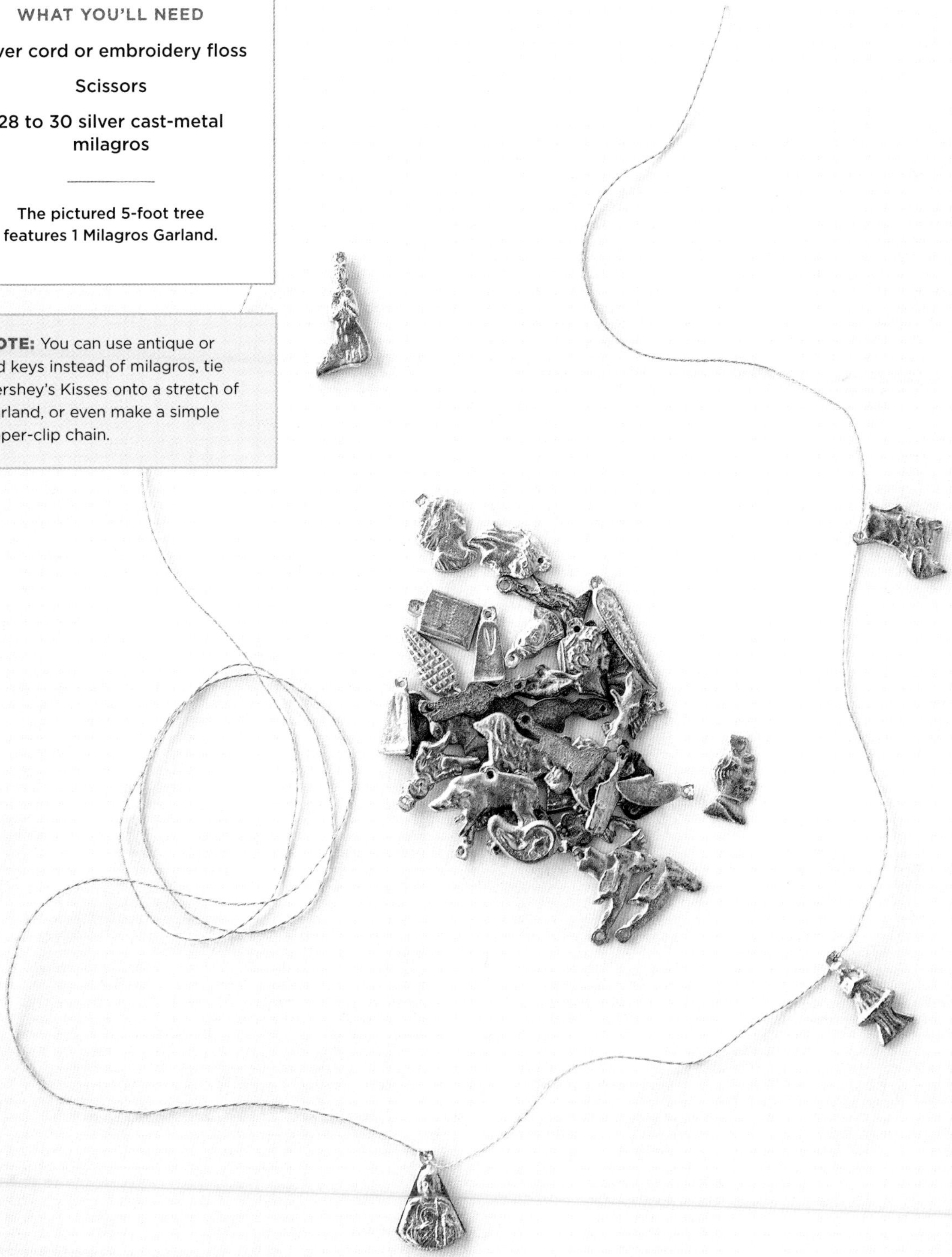

Hang some of the found objects and ornaments with long pieces of cord or ribbon.

2 Tie other objects directly to the branches. Some objects may be too heavy and tip the tree. Add items with care to maintain the overall balance.

3 Perch or lodge some items on the tree trunk or branches.

4 Stick the lichen into the branches and add a few wisps of delicate moss.

BLUE, BLUE CHRISTMAS TREE

Inspired by male satin bowerbirds, which decorate their nests with anything they can steal in shades of blue—from bits of paper, money, and shiny foil to clothespins and plastic debris—this tree celebrates the electric power of true blue! You can add to the blue arsenal by painting objects of other colors in Yves Klein or other shades of blue, as I did with the tin topper I used for this tree. Combine blown-glass Christmas ornaments with your own quirky trinkets and let the incongruous elements sing together!

TREE
White or blue spruce

VESSEL
Stand draped with
a woven blue
rebozo (shawl)

LIGHTS
2 strands of all-blue
large bulbs wound out
to the branch tips;
1 strand of all-blue small
incandescent bulbs
wound deep in the tree

TOPPER
Vintage punched tin star,
painted blue (page 135)

UNDER THE TREE
Large cobalt-blue
mercury glass ball and
vintage calico blue cat

COLLECT
SMALL
ALL-BLUE
INCANDESCENT
LIGHTS

COLLECT
ALL-BLUE
BULB
LIGHTS

COLLECT
MERCURY
GLASS
ORNAMENTS

COLLECT
BLUE CORD

MAKE
CUTOUT BLUE BIRDS
(page 134)

MAKE
PAINTED OBJECTS
(page 135)

COLLECT
BLUE FOUND OBJECTS

Franciscan Studies
St. Bonaventure
P.O. St. Bonaventure
New York N.Y.
U.S.A.

COLLECT

Woven blue **rebozo (shawl)** from Pátzcuaro Michoacán, or any vibrant blue fabric

Vintage and contemporary **mercury glass ornaments** in assorted shapes, sizes, and shades of blue

Assorted blue **found objects.** A few ideas: old airmail letters, plastic comb, rubber beetle, Russian toy soldiers, ceramic teacup, rabbit foot, pencil, ballpoint pen, card, feathers, paper money, blue eggs, strands of glass beads, eyeglasses, passport.

Blue **cord, slender ribbon, or raffia**

MAKE

CUTOUT BLUE BIRDS

WHAT YOU'LL NEED

Bird template (download
at artisanbooks.com/
newxmastree)

Computer and printer

Card stock in various shades of
blue, plain or patterned

Scissors

Silver pen, white colored pencil,
or soft graphite pencil

Hole punch

Blue ribbon, cord, or raffia

The pictured 5-foot tree features
5 Cutout Blue Birds.

1 Print the template on assorted card stock and cut out the birds. Outline and detail the birds with a silver pen, a white colored pencil, or a graphite pencil.

2 To hang, punch holes in the top center of the birds, thread ribbon, cord, or raffia through the holes, and tie the ends together.

MAKE

PAINTED OBJECTS & TOPPER

WHAT YOU'LL NEED

Newspaper

Wooden objects like clothespins or spools

Blue tempera paint and paintbrush or blue spray paint

Star topper (made of tin or another material)

Blue ribbon or raffia

The pictured 5-foot tree features 5 painted objects.

1 Cover your work surface with newspaper. Paint the objects blue with tempera or spray paint. It may take several coats to completely cover the chosen object to the desired depth of color. Let dry.

 To hang the objects, tie ribbon or raffia around them and tie them onto the tree.

MATCHSTICK RED TREE

Chinese New Year meets Christmas on this incendiary all-red themed tree. Fire-related Chinese joss-paper garlands, firecrackers, and matchstick stars patterned after tramp art hang next to vintage Christmas ornaments. Add unexpected found objects like hearts and diamonds from a deck of cards and an old *Plan de Paris* and handmade objects like rubber-band balls in all shades of red. The sum total is a cheery Christmas tree with festive, multilayered cultural references that resonate together.

TREE
White fir, or any
dense tree

VESSEL
Red vintage cast-iron
tree stand

LIGHTS
2 strands of large red
bulbs, loosely wound
in and out to the
branch tips

TOPPER
Red paper diamond,
stuck in the top
branch (or your choice
of small object)

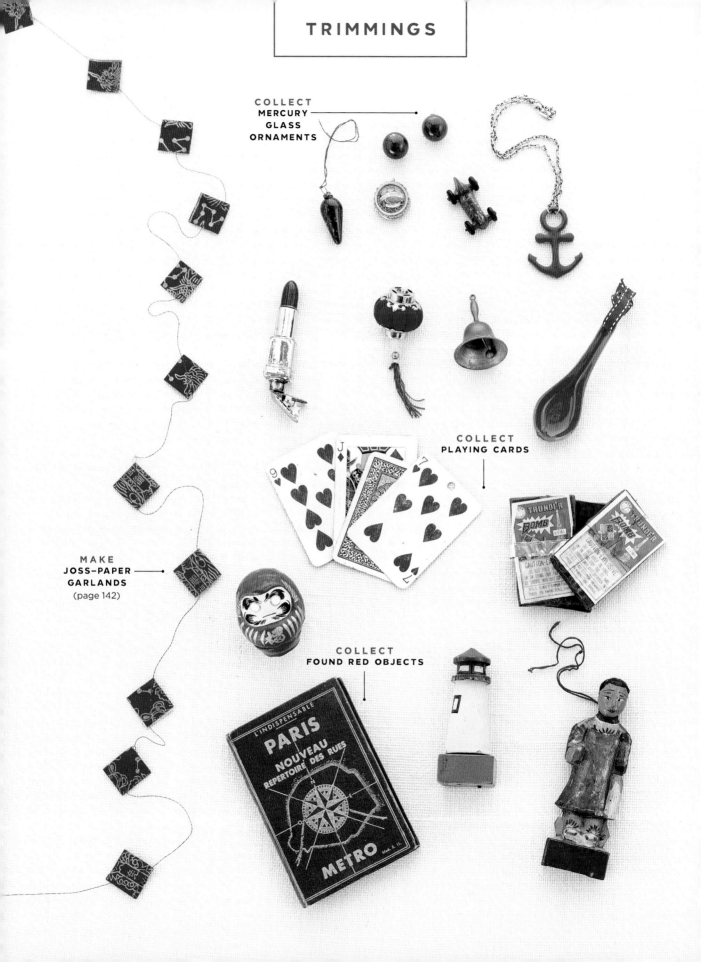

TRIMMINGS

COLLECT
**MERCURY
GLASS
ORNAMENTS**

COLLECT
PLAYING CARDS

MAKE
**JOSS-PAPER
GARLANDS**
(page 142)

COLLECT
FOUND RED OBJECTS

L'INDISPENSABLE
PARIS
NOUVEAU
REPERTOIRE DES RUES
METRO

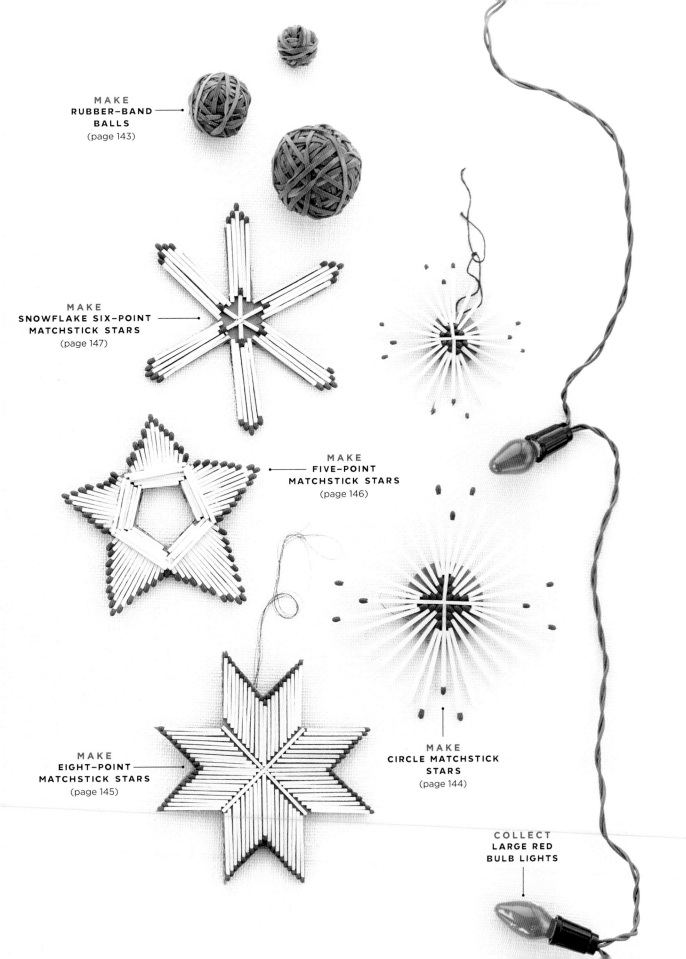

MAKE
RUBBER-BAND
BALLS
(page 143)

MAKE
SNOWFLAKE SIX-POINT
MATCHSTICK STARS
(page 147)

MAKE
FIVE-POINT
MATCHSTICK STARS
(page 146)

MAKE
EIGHT-POINT
MATCHSTICK STARS
(page 145)

MAKE
CIRCLE MATCHSTICK
STARS
(page 144)

COLLECT
LARGE RED
BULB LIGHTS

COLLECT

Vintage red mercury glass ornaments in assorted shapes and sizes. I've found a clip-on lipstick, teardrops, pendants, and assorted bell shapes in addition to traditional spheres.

Playing cards, red suits only (just punch holes at the top and hang them from ornament hooks)

Little packages of **firecrackers and decorative Chinese lanterns**

Found and purchased **red objects**—my finds have included a calico owl with pinecone eyes and a book of red matches (tie the objects onto the tree with red thread, ribbon, or cord)

MAKE

JOSS-PAPER GARLANDS

WHAT YOU'LL NEED

Twenty-eight 10¼-by-9¾-inch sheets of red- and gold-printed joss paper

Scissors

Straightedge or paper cutter

Red thread

Needle or sewing machine

The pictured 4-foot tree features 1 small and 3 large Joss-Paper Garlands.

NOTE: Chinese joss papers are used for burnt offerings to honor ancestors on holidays and at funerals. They can be purchased online or at Asian markets.

1   Trim the joss paper into 1-inch squares, approximately 48 for a 2-yard garland, and 3-inch squares, approximately 216 (shown) for 12 yards of large garlands.

2   Stack pairs of squares together, right sides out. Sew the stacked squares on the diagonal from corner to corner; leave 3 to 4 inches of thread in between each 1-inch square and ½ inch of thread between each 3-inch square.

3   To hang, drape the garlands on the tree as desired, with the smaller garland at the top of the tree and the larger ones in the middle and at the bottom.

MAKE

RUBBER-BAND BALLS

WHAT YOU'LL NEED

Styrofoam balls in 1-inch, 2-inch, and 3-inch sizes

Red rubber bands

Wire hangers, purchased or handmade (see "Making Your Own Ornament Hangers," page 287)

The pictured 4-foot tree features 3 small, 3 medium, and 3 large Rubber-Band Balls.

 Wrap rubber bands around a Styrofoam ball, changing direction with each band until you have completely covered the ball. It should look like a tightly wound ball of twine.

2 To hang, slip an ornament hanger or S-hook under a rubber-band strand.

MAKE

MATCHSTICK STARS

WHAT YOU'LL NEED

Star templates (download at artisanbooks.com/newxmastree)

Computer, printer, and printer paper

Pencil

Cardboard or heavy tag board

Scissors

Utility knife

Large red-tipped wood matches

Clear-drying glue

22-gauge galvanized wire

Masking tape

Red thread or embroidery floss

FOR THE FIVE-POINT STARS:

Straightedge

FOR THE SIX-POINT STARS:

Small red-tipped wood matches

The pictured 4-foot tree features 5 Matchstick Stars.

CIRCLE MATCHSTICK STARS

Trace a 1½-inch circle onto a piece of cardboard and cut it out. Glue four matches in a cross shape, red tips out.

2 Glue four matches between the spokes of the cross, red tips in, to form an X.

3 Glue two matches on either side of all four spokes of the X, red tips in. Glue one match on each side of all four spokes of the cross, red tips out. To hang, tie a red thread around one of the crossed matches or secure a loop of wire on the back with a piece of tape and hang with red thread.

Print the template and cut it out. Trace the design onto cardboard and cut out the star shape using a utility knife.

Using the utility knife, trim the red-tip heads off four matches to glue into an X in the center of the star.

Glue matches, red tips out, to fill in each of the four sections of the star.

To hang, attach a loop of wire to the back of the star with a piece of tape and hang with red thread.

1 | Print the template and cut it out. Trace it onto cardboard and cut out the shape. Use a straightedge to draw pentagon guidelines between each star point.

2 | Using a utility knife, trim five matches to frame the pentagon opening and five to fit the guidelines. Glue them in place.

 Trim matches to fit and fill in each point of the star, retaining the red tips. Glue in place.

4 | Add trimmed matches to fill in the pentagon borders. Stack a second layer on the outside of the pentagon to add dimension. To hang, attach a loop of wire to the back of the star with a piece of tape and hang with red thread.

1 | Print the template and cut it out. Trace it onto cardboard and cut out the shape using a utility knife. Trim six large matches to ¾-inch lengths to make a star in the center, red tips out (the tips should extend into the spokes of the star). Glue them in place.

2 Glue a match in the center of each spoke, lining it up with the center star. Continue to glue matches to fill in the spokes; the tips should extend beyond the cardboard backing.

3 Layer three small-size matches on top of each spoke, following the point pattern; take care not to hide the red tips of the center star. Glue them in place. Glue a fourth match on top of the three, staggering the tips so all four are seen.

4 Using the utility knife, trim small pieces of matchsticks to fill in the space around the center star and glue them in place. Cut the red tips off larger matches and glue them in the center, standing the heads up. To hang, make a loop out of wire and secure it to the back of the star with tape. Hang with red thread.

COPPER & CORK TREE

Revive Christmas colorways with a contemporary palette of copper and cork, accented by shades of celery, chartreuse, and lime green. Every ornament on this tree is handcrafted, combining materials from hardware and art stores to create ornaments with a slightly industrial, Arts-and-Crafts–era-meets-the-Atomic-Age feel. American folk art–inspired penny mosaics and Japanese cut-paper kirigami craft add another layer of pan-cultural references. Admire the rich interplay of textures and colors glowing warmly in winter's light.

TREE
White pine, or any tree
with strong horizontal
branches

VESSEL
Copper urn

LIGHTS
Small gold
incandescent bulbs
wound deep in the
tree and out to some
of the branch tips

TOPPER
Penny Mosaic Star
(page 164)

**MAKE
PENNY MOSAIC
STAR TOPPER**
(page 164)

**MAKE
PENNY MOSAIC
STARS**
(page 163)

**MAKE
WINE-CORK
GARLANDS**
(page 154)

**MAKE
COPPER &
CORK FLOWERS**
(page 159)

**MAKE
TEARDROP
ORNAMENTS**
(page 160)

**MAKE
KIRIGAMI BLOSSOMS**
(page 158)

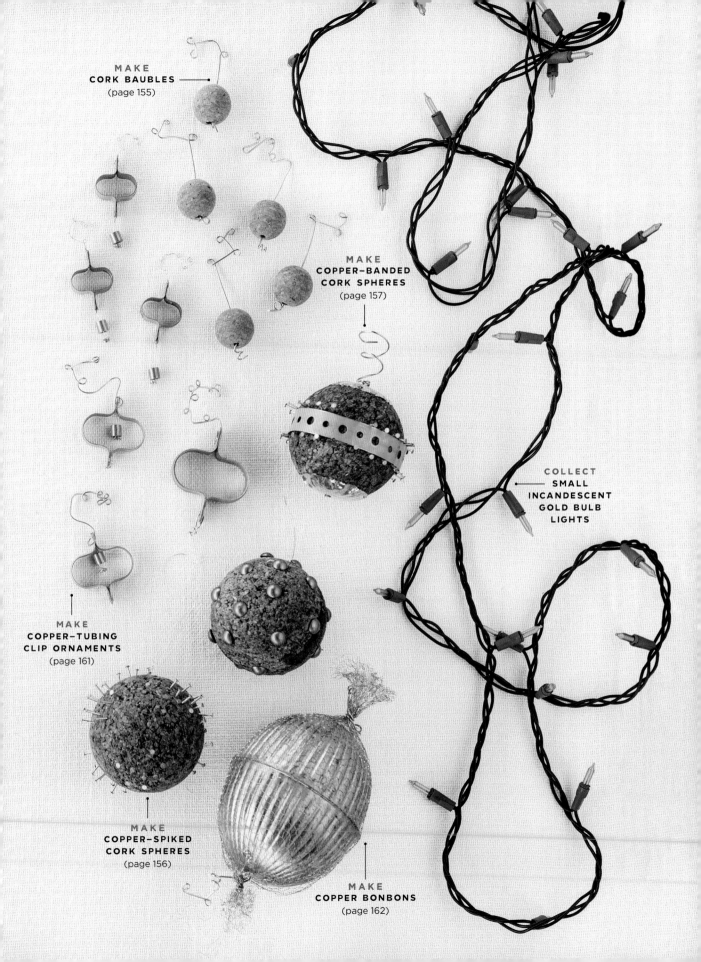

MAKE
CORK BAUBLES
(page 155)

MAKE
**COPPER-BANDED
CORK SPHERES**
(page 157)

COLLECT
**SMALL
INCANDESCENT
GOLD BULB
LIGHTS**

MAKE
**COPPER-TUBING
CLIP ORNAMENTS**
(page 161)

MAKE
**COPPER-SPIKED
CORK SPHERES**
(page 156)

MAKE
COPPER BONBONS
(page 162)

MAKE

WINE-CORK GARLANDS

WHAT YOU'LL NEED

20-gauge copper wire

Wire snips

Round-nose pliers

115 to 125 wine corks

The pictured 4-foot tree features 3 Wine-Cork Garlands.

1. Cut approximately two hundred fifty ¾-inch wire pieces. Bend a loop at one end of each wire with round-nose pliers.

2. Interlock the looped ends by slipping one loop into the other. Pierce the straight end of the wire into the end of a wine cork. Use pliers to open the loops if necessary and to close both loops after interlocking.

3. Continue to add corks to the garland to achieve the desired length. Make multiple strands for different locations, such as the top, middle, and lower portions of the tree; they don't have to be full-circle or continuous-spiral garlands.

MAKE

CORK BAUBLES

WHAT YOU'LL NEED

22-gauge copper wire

Wire snips

1½-inch cork beads

Round-nose pliers

The pictured 4-foot tree features
5 Cork Baubles.

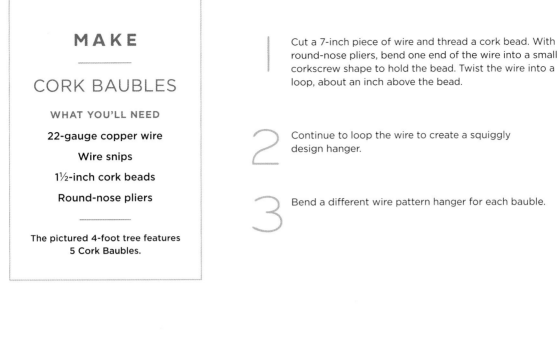

1 Cut a 7-inch piece of wire and thread a cork bead. With round-nose pliers, bend one end of the wire into a small corkscrew shape to hold the bead. Twist the wire into a loop, about an inch above the bead.

2 Continue to loop the wire to create a squiggly design hanger.

3 Bend a different wire pattern hanger for each bauble.

MAKE

EMBELLISHED CORK SPHERES

WHAT YOU'LL NEED

3-inch cork balls

Hammer

Wire snips

FOR THE SPIKED SPHERES:

¾-inch copper weather-stripping nails

26-gauge copper wire

FOR THE STUDDED SPHERES:

Copper or brass upholstery tacks

Metallic copper paint (optional)

Small paintbrush (optional)

26-gauge copper wire

FOR THE BANDED SPHERES:

Copper strapping tape

Metal cutters

¾-inch copper cut tacks

3 mm–thick copper sheet

Titanium scissors

Ballpoint pen

¾-inch copper weather-stripping nails

20-gauge copper wire

Round-nose pliers

The pictured 4-foot tree features 6 Cork Spheres.

COPPER-SPIKED CORK SPHERES

1 Hammer copper weather-stripping nails into a cork ball in spiky clusters.

2 Wrap a 4-inch length of 26-gauge copper wire around one of the nails and make a loop to hang.

COPPER-STUDDED CORK SPHERES

1 Hammer upholstery tacks into a cork ball; make lines or random patterns.

2 Pound one tack halfway in at the top for the wire hanger.

3 If you're using brass upholstery tacks, carefully paint them with copper paint. Attach a 4-inch 26-gauge copper wire loop to the top tack for hanging.

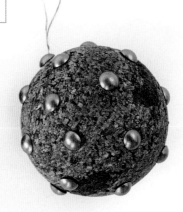

COPPER-BANDED CORK SPHERES

1 | Measure, then use metal cutters to cut a length of copper strapping tape to fit the circumference of the cork ball. Hammer cut tacks halfway into the cork, through every other hole in the strapping, to secure it in place. Continue to hammer tacks inside or outside of the strapping tape in a decorative pattern.

 Draw two 2¼-inch circles on the copper sheet and cut them out using titanium scissors. Center them on the top and bottom of the cork ball, and hammer a tack through the center of each sheet (halfway in the top, all the way into the bottom).

3 | Hammer weather-stripping nails around the edge of each round—it's fine if the metal puckers a little.

 Cut a 3-inch length of 20-gauge copper wire and wind it around the top tack. Use round-nose pliers to twist it in a decorative loop to make a hanger.

MAKE

KIRIGAMI BLOSSOMS

WHAT YOU'LL NEED

Sheets of green rice or art paper

Kirigami flower templates (download at artisanbooks.com/newxmastree)

Computer, printer, and printer paper

Pencil

Scissors

One 18-inch-by-4-foot roll of ⅛-inch-thick self-adhesive cork

Two 9-by-12-inch sheets of decorative patterned copper paper (or one 19-by-25-inch sheet)

One 12-by-24-inch roll of 32-gauge copper sheet

Hammer and finishing nail

⅛-inch copper brads

Metallic copper fat-tipped marker pen (optional)

26-gauge copper wire

The pictured 4-foot tree features 5 Kirigami Blossoms.

Cut a kirigami flower out of a 4-inch square of green rice paper (see "Making a Kirigami Flower," page 288). Print the large, medium, and small kirigami flower ornament templates and cut them out. Adhere green rice paper to the back of a piece of cork that fits the large template. Trace the large template onto the green paper and cut it out. Trace the medium-size template onto decorative copper paper and cut it out. Trace the small template onto a copper sheet and cut it out.

2 Stack the four cutout pieces in graduating sizes, offsetting the petals of each piece. Punch a hole through the center with a hammer and finishing nail.

3 Poke a copper brad through the hole and fasten. Use a metallic copper marker to outline the outer edges, if desired. To hang, pierce a hole with the hammer and nail through the cork at the top and hang with a loop of copper wire.

MAKE

COPPER & CORK FLOWERS

WHAT YOU'LL NEED

Flower templates (optional; download at artisanbooks.com/newxmastree)

Computer, printer, and printer paper (optional)

Scissors

Ballpoint pen

3 mm–thick copper sheet

Titanium scissors

One 18-inch-by-4-foot roll of ⅛-inch-thick self-adhesive cork

Hammer and nail

Nail punch

Tiny copper brads

26-gauge copper wire

Stylus (optional)

Rice or art papers in shades of light green (optional)

The pictured 4-foot tree features 5 Copper & Cork Flowers.

NOTE: You can draw and stipple decorations on the copper backs of the flowers using a stylus for further decoration.

1. Print four sizes of flower templates and cut them out. You can also draw your own; a flower cookie cutter makes a good starting template, then you need to sketch a larger flower and two smaller flower templates to match. Use a ballpoint pen to trace the largest and second-smallest flower templates onto copper and cut them out with titanium scissors. Trace the second-largest and the smallest flower templates onto cork and cut them out.

2. Stack the cork and copper flowers in graduated sizes, and glue each to the flower below.

3. Punch a hole in the center of the flower with a hammer and nail. Insert a copper brad and fasten. Bend the copper petals to finish creating the flower.

4. To hang, punch a hole through one of the petals and make a loop with 26-gauge copper wire. Make a variety of flowers, alternating copper, cork, and rice paper in different combinations.

MAKE

TEARDROP ORNAMENTS

WHAT YOU'LL NEED

Teardrop templates (download at artisanbooks.com/newxmastree)

Computer, printer, and printer paper

Scissors

One 19-by-25-inch sheet of green art paper

One 18-inch-by-4-foot roll of ⅛-inch-thick self-adhesive cork

Pencil

Metallic copper fat-tipped marker or metallic copper paint and fine paintbrush (optional)

Hammer and finishing nail

26-gauge copper wire

The pictured 4-foot tree features 5 teardrop ornaments.

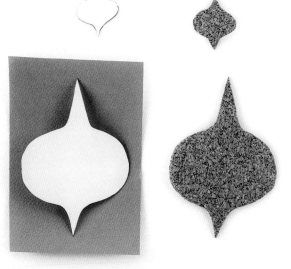

1 Print the large and small ornament templates and cut them out. Adhere the green paper to a piece of cork large enough to fit the large template. Trace the large template onto this paper and cut it out. Trace the small template onto a separate piece of cork and cut it out.

2 Adhere the small cork shape to the green paper side of the ornament.

3 Decorate the edges of the shapes with copper marker or copper paint, adding a few brushstrokes for further embellishment if you like. To hang, pierce the top of the ornament with a finishing nail, and hang with a loop of copper wire. Make a variety of ornaments using different combinations of cork and paper.

MAKE

COPPER-TUBING CLIP ORNAMENTS

WHAT YOU'LL NEED

Copper tubing clips in three sizes: ½-inch, ¾-inch, and 1-inch (you'll need two for each ornament)

26-gauge copper wire

Wire snips

Needle-nose pliers

⅛-inch stop-sleeve copper "beads"

20-gauge copper wire

The pictured 4-foot tree features 8 Copper-Tubing Clip Ornaments, using the three sizes of clips (with a different hanger for each one).

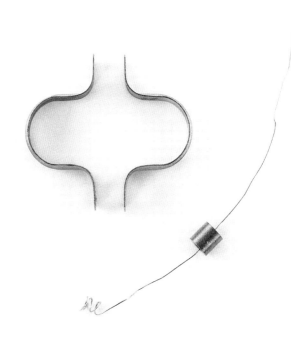

Match up two copper tubing clips of the same size and arrange them so that the flat "feet" touch and the holes line up. Cut a 3½-inch piece of 26-gauge copper wire. Wrap one end of the wire tightly around needle-nose pliers and make a little corkscrew that is larger than the hole in the copper bead. Slide the wire off the pliers and string the bead.

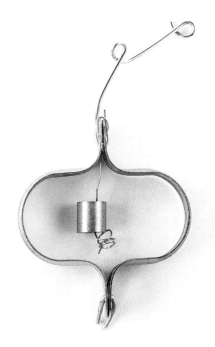

2 Thread the wire from the inside out through one of the holes at the "top" of the copper tubing clip. Pull the wire until the bead is centered between the two clips. Close the clips together and repeatedly loop the wire around the top of the ornament and through both holes to fasten. Trim the excess wire.

3 Fasten the bottom two holes together with a 2-inch piece of 20-gauge copper wire. Trim off the excess wire. Thread a 6-inch length of 20-gauge copper wire through the top holes and wrap it to fasten in place. Use the pliers to bend loops back and forth to make a whimsical hanger.

MAKE

COPPER BONBONS

WHAT YOU'LL NEED

1 copper scrubby pad for each bonbon

1 copper float (found at hardware stores) for each bonbon

22-gauge copper wire

Wire snips

Round-nose pliers

The pictured 4-foot tree features 3 Copper Bonbons.

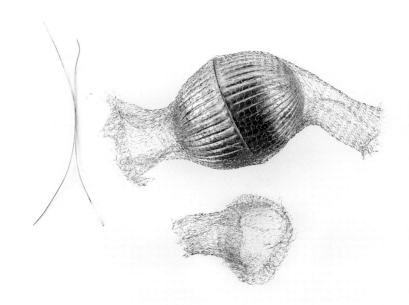

Unroll the copper scrubby into a tube and slip the copper float inside. Position the float 3 or 4 inches from one end of the tube, and cut the other end to match.

2 Wrap an 8-inch length of copper wire tightly around one end of the bonbon. Use pliers to secure it and bend both ends of the wire in decorative curly loops.

3 Repeat on the other end of the bonbon. Nestle the bonbon in the lower branches of the tree or hang it from a branch with a 4-inch length of wire attached to one end of the bonbon.

MAKE

PENNY MOSAIC STARS

WHAT YOU'LL NEED

Six-Point Star templates (download at artisanbooks .com/newxmastree)

Computer, printer, and printer paper

Scissors

One 19-by-25-inch piece of rice or art paper in a shade of green

One 18-inch-by-4-foot roll of ⅛-inch-thick self-adhesive cork

Pencil

Pinking shears

18 pennies

Glue, Duco, or similar metal adhesive

Hammer and finishing nail

26-gauge copper wire

The pictured 4-foot tree features 5 Penny Mosaic Stars.

Print the midsize and the small Six-Point Star templates and cut them out. Adhere green rice or art paper to the back of a piece of cork large enough to fit the midsize star. Trace the template onto it. Trace the small star template onto another piece of cork.

2 Cut out both stars with pinking shears. Adhere the smaller cork star on top of the green-paper side of the larger star.

3 Glue pennies to the back (cork side) of the larger star; then stack a second layer of pennies in the center of the star. Allow to dry overnight. To hang, punch a hole with a hammer and a finishing nail between two of the points and hang with an 8-inch length of copper wire.

MAKE

PENNY MOSAIC
STAR TOPPER

WHAT YOU'LL NEED

Six-Point Star templates
(download at artisanbooks
.com/newxmastree)

Computer, printer, and printer paper

Scissors

Pencil

32-gauge copper sheet

Pinking shears

One 18-inch-by-4-foot roll of
⅛-inch-thick self-adhesive cork

One 20-by-30-inch piece of
black foam core or mat board

Straightedge and utility knife

One 8½-by-11-inch sheet of rice
or art paper in a shade of green

Glue, Duco or similar
metal adhesive

Pennies

Flat wooden ice cream spoon

Metallic copper paint and
small paintbrush

22-gauge copper wire

Wire snips

26-gauge copper wire
(optional)

Print out the four sizes of the Six-Point Star templates
and cut them out. Trace the largest template onto copper
and second-largest template onto cork and cut them out
with pinking shears. Trace the third-largest template onto
black foam core and smallest template onto green rice
or art paper and cut them out with a straightedge and a
utility knife. Adhere the sticky side of the cork star to
the black star.

4 Paint one side of a flat wooden ice cream spoon with
copper paint. Allow to dry. Coil 22-gauge copper
wire tightly around the spoon and twist at the top
to secure it in place. Extend the coil a few inches
beyond the spoon, and cut the end with wire snips.

2 Glue the black star to the copper star, offsetting the points of both stars. Glue the green paper star to the cork star, once again offsetting the points.

3 Glue pennies in a star pattern on top of the green and cork stars. Allow to dry overnight.

5 Press the spoon firmly against the wire coil on a flat surface to flatten the wire. Glue the spoon to the back of the copper star, in line with two of the star points. Allow to dry overnight.

6 To hang, slip the coiled wire over the top branch of the tree. Secure the coil in place with a length of 26-gauge wire if necessary.

PAPERWHITE TREE

Cover this tree in fluttering winter-white decorations inspired by *papel picados,* the popular cut-paper banners and flags used in Mexico for all fiesta occasions. This is a study in texture, using every conceivable paper weight from delicate tissue, embossed rice, and transparent tracing to stretchy crepe and heavy cotton rag. Ethereal string spheres and origami lanterns defuse the lights. Top this confection with a bouquet finial.

TREE

Douglas fir, or any
very full tree

VESSEL

Stand draped in
black velvet

LIGHTS

Mini incandescent
white lights, some
covered with
Origami Light Shades
(page 172) and others
with Spun-String
Spheres (page 174)

TOPPER

Finial Bouquet
(page 182)

TRIMMINGS

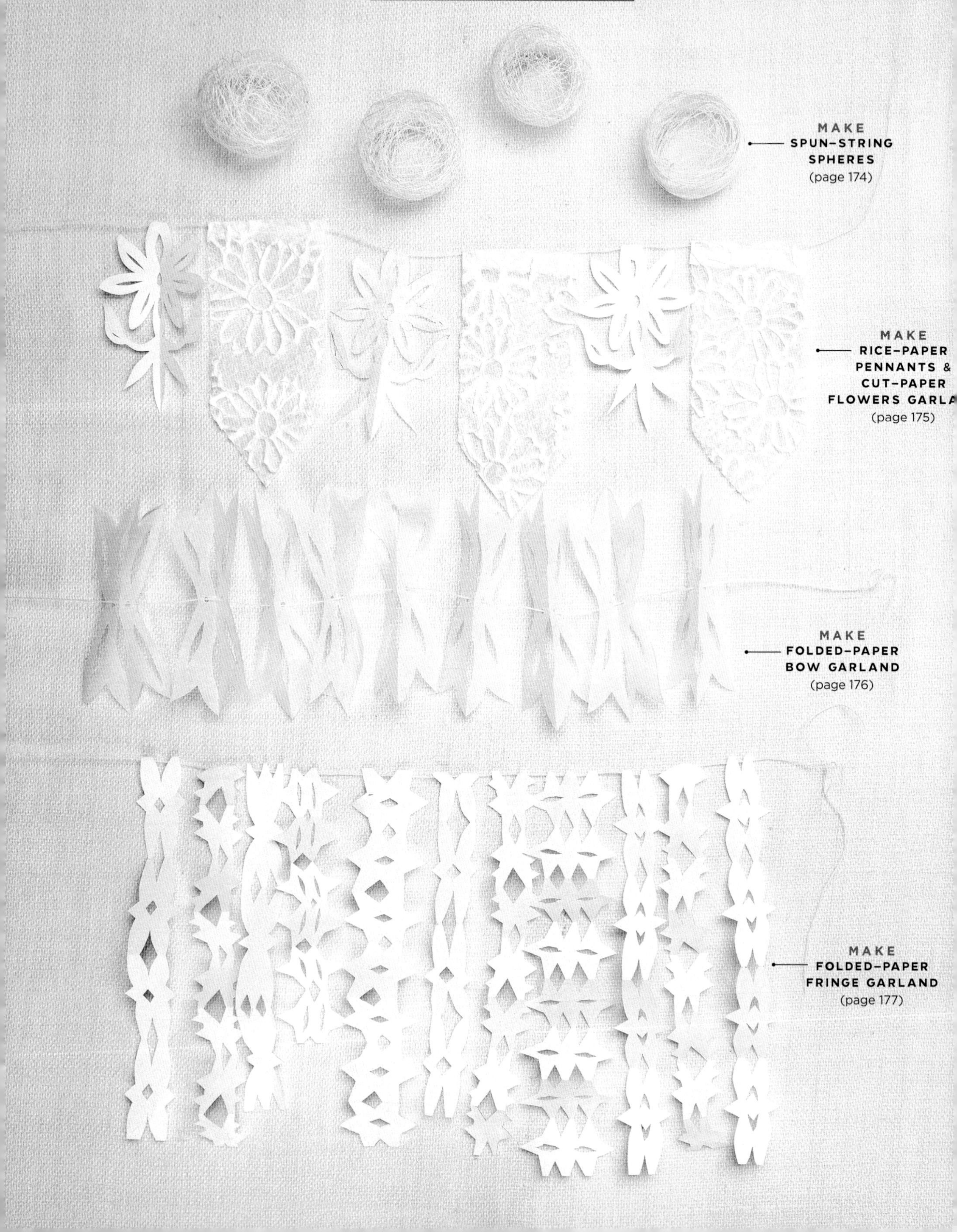

MAKE
**SPUN–STRING
SPHERES**
(page 174)

MAKE
**RICE–PAPER
PENNANTS &
CUT–PAPER
FLOWERS GARLA**
(page 175)

MAKE
**FOLDED–PAPER
BOW GARLAND**
(page 176)

MAKE
**FOLDED–PAPER
FRINGE GARLAND**
(page 177)

MAKE
CREPE-PAPER
ROSES
(page 180)

MAKE
ORIGAMI LIGHT
SHADES
(page 172)

MAKE
CREPE-PAPER VINES
(page 179)

MAKE
CREPE-PAPER POPPIES
(page 181)

COLLECT
MINI INCANDESCENT
WHITE LIGHTS

MAKE
PAPER POINSETTIAS
(page 178)

MAKE

ORIGAMI LIGHT SHADES

WHAT YOU'LL NEED

1 package of 4-inch white origami paper squares, or rice paper cut into 4-inch squares

---

The pictured 6-foot tree features 40 Origami Light Shades.

Fold a square in half on the diagonal. Unfold. Repeat on the opposite diagonal.

5   Fold the top layer of the outer-left corner to the center point. Turn the square over and repeat steps 4 and 5.

6   You now have a diamond shape. Fold the top layer of the right corner to the center.

7   Repeat the fold on the left side; turn over and repeat the same two folds.

2 Fold in half to make a rectangle. Crease and unfold.

3 Collapse the prefolded square, pinching the centers of the rectangle fold together, resulting in a folded triangle shape.

4 Fold the top layer of the outer-right corner of the triangle up to the center point.

8 Fold each of the top points back onto themselves and dog-ear the points. Tuck each bent point into the pockets of the previous folds.

9 Crease the tucked flaps neatly into the pockets. Repeat on the other side and crease.

10 Blow up the origami shade like a balloon. To string: After the lights are on the tree, place the shades on the lights you choose to cover, inserting the light into the shade hole.

MAKE

SPUN-STRING SPHERES

WHAT YOU'LL NEED

Balloons

Heavy-weight
white cotton thread
(the thread *must* be cotton)

Scissors

Spray starch

Clothesline or a place to
hang the balloons

The pictured 6-foot tree features
5 Spun-String Spheres.

NOTE: For the Finial Bouquet
Topper on page 182, create a
3- to 4-inch tall cylinder version
with a 2½- to 3-inch opening at
both ends of the balloon. Wrap the
string in one direction, overlapping
back and forth, around the center
of the balloon only.

Blow up each balloon to about the size of a baseball. Tie
a length of thread to the end for hanging. Shake the can
of spray starch and cover the balloon with starch.

2 Wrap the thread around and around the balloon,
overlapping many times and going every which
way. Saturate the thread-covered balloon with
spray starch and hang to dry overnight.

3 When the thread is completely dry and firm
to the touch, pop the balloon and remove it
from the center of the thread sphere. To hang,
delicately place the thread sphere over a bulb
on the tree (choose prime locations!). Relocate
origami shades if necessary.

MAKE

PAPER GARLANDS

WHAT YOU'LL NEED

Garland templates (download at artisanbooks .com/newxmastree)

Computer, printer, and printer paper

Utility knife

Paper scissors

Decorative rice papers (several 26-by-38-inch sheets), tracing paper or vellum (one 9-by-12-inch pad), and white letter-weight paper (one 9-by-12-inch pad)

Paper clips (optional)

Small hole punch

White waxed string

Clear-drying glue

The pictured 6-foot tree features 3 Paper Garlands, 1 in each style.

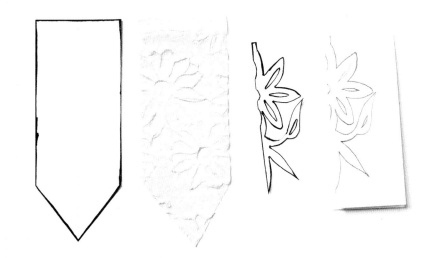

Print the pennant and folded flower templates. Use a utility knife to cut the flower interior and scissors to cut along the outline. Trace the pennant design onto decorative rice paper and cut each pennant separately. Make multiple pennants, two per foot of garland. Fold a piece of letter-weight paper in half and trace the flower design along the fold. Use scissors and the utility knife to cut out multiple flowers, one per foot of garland.

2 Cut a piece of string long enough to drape around the midsection of the tree. Fold the tops of the paper shapes over the waxed string, alternating pennants and flowers. Glue the paper to itself, not to the string, so you can slide the shapes on the string to position them.

3 To hang, drape around the tree, adjusting the individual pieces to space them evenly.

FOLDED-PAPER BOWS

1 Print the bow template. Cut along the outline with scissors and cut out the interior shapes with a utility knife. Fold multiple sheets of tracing paper or vellum in half; if you like, use paper clips to securely hold the papers together. Trace the template onto the paper and cut out the pieces. Your finished garland should be long enough to wrap once around the top third of your tree, with a few deep swags—cut approximately twelve bows per foot.

2 Punch a hole in the center of the folded bows. Separate the bows.

3 String the bows on waxed string.

4 To hang, drape around the tree and adjust the individual bows between the branches; they will flutter in different directions.

1 | Print out templates of multiple fringe shapes. Cut along the outline with scissors and cut out the interior shapes with a utility knife. Cut multiple strips of letter-weight paper commensurate with the width of each design you choose. You can vary the length of each fringe piece or make them approximately the same. Accordion-fold each strip to match the height of the selected shape.

2 | Trace each design onto the folded paper.

3 | Cut out the design using scissors and the utility knife. Cut a length of waxed string long enough to drape around the bottom of the tree, and create enough fringe strips to fill it, spaced about ½ inch apart.

4 | Fold the tops of the strips over the string and glue the paper to itself, not the string, so you can slide the strips into position. Alternate the fringe patterns. To hang, stretch the fringe around the bottom of the tree, and adjust the individual strips.

MAKE

PAPER POINSETTIAS

WHAT YOU'LL NEED

1 large sheet of white
heavy-weight rag paper
(approximately
26 by 36 inches)

Scissors

Straightedge

Bone folder

Small hole punch

White florist wire

Wire snips

Hot glue gun and glue sticks

White floral tape

Clear-drying glue

White superfine glitter
(optional)

The pictured 6-foot tree
features 3 Paper Poinsettias.

Cut fifteen ½-inch- to 2-inch-wide strips of white heavy-weight rag paper. Use a straightedge and a bone folder to crisply fold the strips in half. Cut petal shapes ranging in sizes from 2 to 4 inches long. You will need five to seven of each size petal for one flower. Hole-punch the scraps and save the punches for decoration (see step 3).

2 Hot-glue a length of white florist wire to the center crease on the back of each petal to extend 2 inches below the petal, and bend to 90 degrees. Gather the wires affixed to the smallest petals and twist them together to create the center of the flower. Gather the next-size petals underneath and twist them around the flower center. Continue until all the petals are arranged as you like.

3 Wrap the wire "stem" with white florist tape. Use white glue to add a few of the punched circles to the innermost petals. Embellish with white superfine glitter, if desired, working over clean sheets of paper so that you can pick up any excess and reuse it. To hang, use the wire stem or additional florist wire to secure the flowers to tree branches.

MAKE

CREPE-PAPER VINES & FLOWERS

WHAT YOU'LL NEED

One roll of heavy white German crepe paper, 20 inches wide by 4 feet long (not a party streamer)

Scissors

White waxed string

White floral tape

White florist wire

The pictured 6-foot tree features 15 Crepe-Paper Flowers and 10 Crepe-Paper Vines.

NOTE: Make different vines by varying the leaf size, spacing, and length.

VINES

1   Cut freehand from crepe paper an odd number of leaves in two sizes, 1½ to 3 inches long. Cut a 14- to 16-inch length of waxed string.

2   With floral tape, attach a large leaf to the string a few inches from the end. Continue to attach the leaves, spacing them a few inches apart. Graduate leaf size from all large to all small.

3   Shape each leaf by stretching the crepe paper with your thumbs. Wind them around groups of flowers or let them dangle gracefully from a branch.

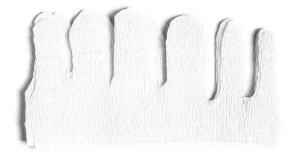

1 | Measure and cut a piece of crepe paper 3½ inches wide and about 35 inches long across the grain. Accordion-fold the paper in 5-inch sections. Draw continuous petals on the folded paper. Cut out the petals.

 Unfold the cut paper and roll it tightly from one end to the other.

3 Wrap the bottom of the petals with floral tape and trim the edge below the tape to neaten.

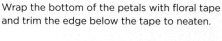 Separate and spread the petals. Nestle or cluster roses in the branches or wrap white floral wire around the flower stem, and wire onto the tree.

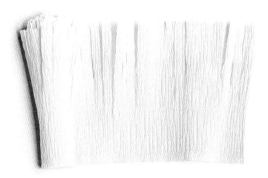

| Measure and cut a piece of crepe paper 3 inches wide and about 25 inches long across the grain. Accordion-fold the paper in 5-inch sections. Cut the fringe along the top, with the grain. Unfold and tightly roll the strip.

2 Wrap a piece of floral tape around the bottom and trim the edge below the tape to neaten.

3 Measure and cut another piece of crepe paper 2½ inches wide and about 25 inches long. Cut the strip across the grain. Accordion-fold the paper in 5-inch sections. Draw continuous petals on the folded paper. Cut out the petals. Wrap the petal roll around the fringe center.

4 Wrap the stem tightly with floral tape; trim. Open and shape the petals. Nestle or cluster the poppies in the branches or wrap floral wire around the flower stem, and wire onto the tree.

MAKE

FINIAL BOUQUET TOPPER

WHAT YOU'LL NEED

Finial and branch templates (download at artisanbooks .com/newxmastree)

Computer, printer, and printer paper

One 20-by-30-inch piece of 24-ply rag card stock or mat board

Pencil

Scissors

One 26-by-36-inch piece of white heavy-weight rag paper

4 to 5 small Crepe-Paper Roses (follow the instructions on page 180, scaling down the roses to 1½ inches)

2 to 3 small Paper Poinsettias (follow the instructions on page 178, scaling down the petals to range in size from ½ inch to 2 inches)

Clear-drying glue

Utility knife

Spun-String Cylinder (see Note, page 174)

White florist wire

Print the finial template. Trace and cut out the shape from the heavy rag card stock. Print the branch template. Trace and cut out three branches from the rag paper. Arrange the roses and poinsettias as you like on the finial template, and cut holes in the template where you want to place the flowers. Arrange the branches and glue into place. Allow to dry.

2 Set the flowers in the cut holes and glue into place. Cut a 2-inch-tall paper loop out of rag paper and glue it to the back of the finial shape to slip over the treetop. Place the Spun-String Cylinder around the bottom of the finial for added decoration. Use white florist wire to further secure the topper in place.

TYPOGRAPHY TREE

What's black and white and re(a)d all over? No, not the newspaper, but a wonderful collection of letters in stylish fonts, both upper- and lowercase, trimmed in silver and glitter on a graphic tree. Evoking Russian Constructivist poster design of the 1920s, in black, white, red, and shades of gray, this is the perfect tree for designers, wordsmiths, and Scrabble players. Spell out *Peace, Love,* and *Joy* to the world!

TREE
Douglas fir, or any tree
with dense foliage

VESSEL
Stand draped in
charcoal-gray velvet

LIGHTS
Small white lights
wound deep in the tree
and out to the branch
tips

TOPPER
Compass Rose
(page 189)

UNDER THE TREE
Gifts embellished
with initials

MAKE
LETTER
ORNAMENTS
(page 188)

GERMAN FANTASY
CAPITALS WITH
DECORATIVE
INTERIORS

ART DECO
VIENNESE
FONTS

SPANISH STRETCHED
TYPE FOR SIGN MAKING

NINETEENTH-
CENTURY BRITISH
WOODCUT & POSTER
BLOCK LETTERS

ALPHABETS
FOUND IN OLD
BOOKS OF TYPE

MAKE

LETTER
ORNAMENTS

WHAT YOU'LL NEED

Computer and printer

Card stock or rag paper in
red, white, black, and assorted
shades of gray

Circle or oval paper cutter,
straightedge and utility knife,
or scissors

Clear-drying glue

Silver glitter and mica

White paper

White and red colored pencils
or china markers (optional)

Metallic silver pens

Red thread

Needle

The pictured 5-foot tree features
65 Letter Ornaments.

1 Search online typography sites like 1001Fonts.com and FontSquirrel.com for interesting typefaces in the public domain with strong graphic appeal. Download fonts and install on your computer. Choose the individual letters you want to print, making sure you select a wide range of the alphabet; you'll definitely want all the vowels. Decide what you want to spell out: words, names, family initials, etc. Try to print letters of a similar scale in small, medium, large, and extra-large, so they hang nicely together in groupings on the tree.

2 Print letters on sheets of colored card stock. Cut out the letters with a circle cutter, an oval cutter, a paper cutter, or a straightedge and a utility knife, or freehand with scissors.

3 Decorate the edges of the letters with glue and glitter, working over a sheet of clean white paper so that you can reuse any excess glitter. You can also hand-color letters, adding shading or details. Use a straightedge and a metallic pen to add borders or to frame. To hang, thread a needle with a spool of red thread and sew through the top of each letter, cutting lengths of thread as you go. Tie the letters on the tree.

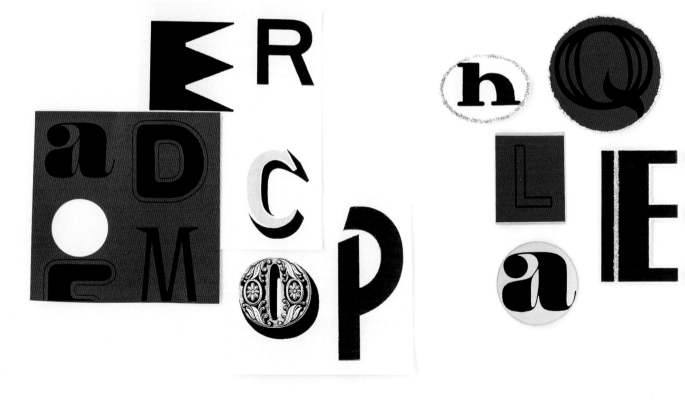

MAKE

COMPASS ROSE TOPPER

WHAT YOU'LL NEED

Computer and printer

Three 8½-by-11-inch sheets each of red, gray, and white card stock

Three 8½-by-11-inch sheets of heavy black card stock

Straightedge and utility knife

One 8-by-10-inch piece of black foam core

Circle cutter or circle template

White paper

Clear-drying glue

Silver or white glitter and mica flakes

Double-sided tape

Cut the following pieces from larger sheets with a straightedge and a utility knife or a paper cutter:

Two 11-by-¼-inch strips of red card stock
One 11-by-¼-inch strip of gray card stock
Two 10-by-¼-inch strips of white card stock
Two 10-by-¼-inch strips of black card stock
Fourteen 1¼-inch-tall triangles in red, white, gray, and black card stock
One 8½-by-11-inch strip of black card stock

Cut the following pieces using a circle cutter and a utility knife:

One 3-inch circle of black foam core
One 4-inch circle of black card stock
One 4-inch circle of black foam core

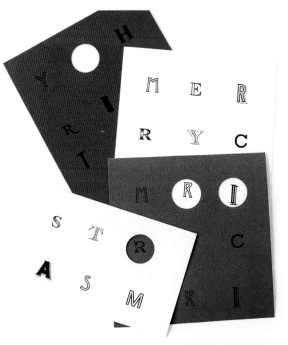

2 Using a few of the typefaces you selected for your letter ornaments (opposite), print the phrase MERRY CHRISTMAS onto red, white, and gray card stock. Try to make each letter about the same size, from 1 to 1¼ inches. Use the circle cutter set on 1½ inches to cut out each letter.

3 Lay sheets of clean white paper on your work surface. Use a small amount of glue to add glitter to some or all of the edges of your letters, as described in step 3 of Letter Ornaments, opposite.

Continued

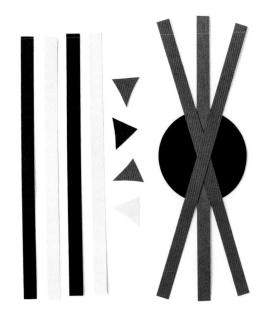

4 Print one large "O" (about 2½ inches tall) on red card stock. Use the circle cutter set on 3 inches to cut out this letter. Embellish the edges with glitter, again working over white paper. Glue your embellished 3-inch circle letter to the 3-inch circle of black foam core. Set it aside to dry.

5 Glue the strip of gray card stock to the center of the black card stock circle. Arrange the red strips in an X over the gray strip and glue them in place.

8 Make a paper cone by rolling up the 8½-by-11-inch piece of black card stock on the diagonal. Use double-sided tape to hold it together at the seam.

9 Trim the bottom to make a 7-inch cone. Embellish the bottom with glitter.

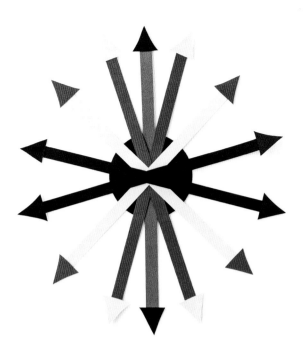

6 Evenly distribute the white and black strips like the spokes of a wheel. Glue the triangle "arrowheads" to the end of each strip. Mix and match colors as you please.

7 Glue the embellished MERRY CHRISTMAS letters just below the "arrowheads." Start with the C at the top. Glue your 3-inch "O" to the center of the compass. Set aside to dry.

10 Flatten the top 3 inches of your paper cone and glue to the 4-inch black foam core circle. Set aside to dry.

11 When everything has completely dried, use double-sided tape to affix the "Merry Christmas" compass to the 4-inch foam core circle. Make sure the letter C is at the top. Slip the cone over the top branch of the tree.

Hang smaller letters at the top, graduating to very large letters at the bottom.

 Spell out words horizontally, diagonally, and vertically on the tree.

3 Fill in gaps with random letters, distributing colors in a pleasing array.

4 Print and embellish letters to decorate packages under the tree. Wrap them in newspaper.

GALAXY TREE

"You are my sun, my moon, and all my stars." —e.e. cummings

All the planets of the solar system, hand-painted and printed, orbit a blazing sun worthy of the Sun King on this tree depicting the cosmos. Enveloped in a Milky Way garland of light-diffusing tulle, it's a virtual Christmas night ablaze with stylized comets, shooting stars, and swirling nebulae. Space illustration of the past meets NASA-powered observation of the future. Timeless.

TREE
White spruce, or any other tree with dense branches

VESSEL
Stand draped in black velvet

LIGHTS
Mini incandescent white lights wound deep in the tree and out to the branch tips; white LED "seed" lights encased in tulle (page 198)

TOPPER
Vintage glitter star

MAKE
PRINTED &
HAND−COLORED
PLANETS
(page 199)

MAKE
COMETS
(page 201)

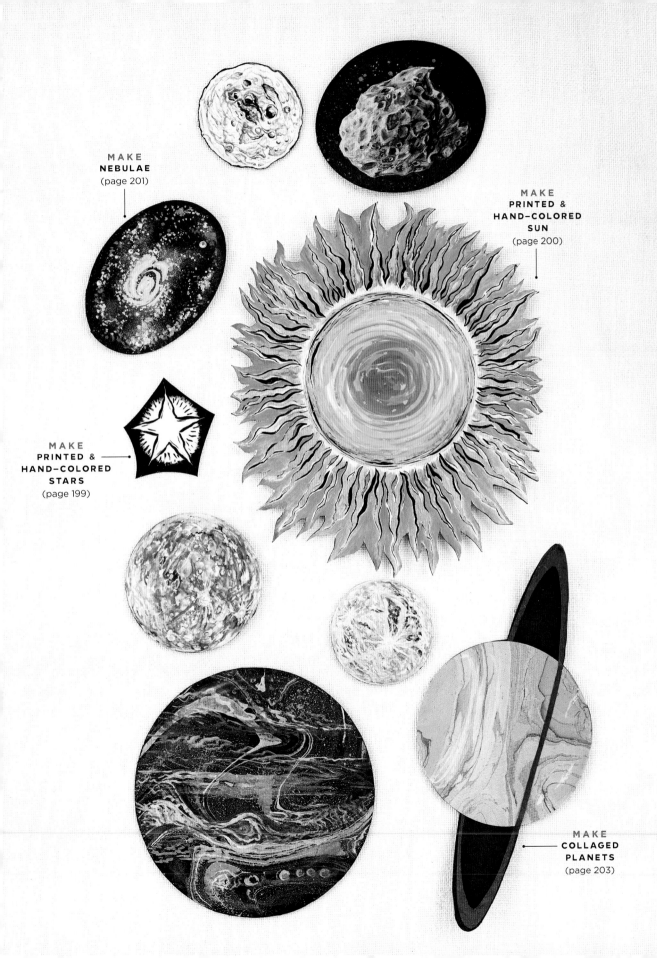

MAKE
NEBULAE
(page 201)

MAKE
**PRINTED &
HAND-COLORED
SUN**
(page 200)

MAKE
**PRINTED &
HAND-COLORED
STARS**
(page 199)

MAKE
**COLLAGED
PLANETS**
(page 203)

MAKE

MILKY WAY GARLAND

WHAT YOU'LL NEED

2 yards of white
fine-weave tulle

Scissors

White polyester thread

Sewing machine or needle for
hand sewing

One 10-foot strand of white
LED "seed" lights

4 yards of off-white tulle

The pictured 6-foot tree
features 1 Milky Way Garland.

1. Cut the yardage of white fine-weave tulle down the
middle lengthwise. You will have two 27-by-72-inch
pieces of tulle.

2. Sew the 27-inch edges together to make one
27-by-144-inch-long piece of tulle.

3. Fold the tulle in half lengthwise; keep the 27-inch
seam on the outside. Sew the opposite ends of the
tulle together to create a 144-inch-long tube.

4. Turn the tube inside out and feed the string of lights
through the tube.

5. After draping the garland on the tree, loosely wrap
the off-white tulle lengthwise around the garland.

MAKE

PRINTED AND HAND-COLORED PLANETS & STARS

WHAT YOU'LL NEED

Solar system ornament templates (download at artisanbooks.com/newxmastree)

Computer, printer, and printer paper or pencil and waterproof ink

Twenty-five 8½-by-11-inch sheets of white archival paper in a smooth finish for inkjet printing

White 100-percent cotton rag paper for painting, 22-by-30-inch loose sheets or a 12-by-16-inch watercolor block (optional)

Circle cutter (optional)

Watercolor set and assorted gouache paint in white, black, ultramarine, and cerulean blue

Watercolor brushes

Scissors (optional)

Utility knife

Clear-drying archival glue or rubber cement

One 20-by-30-inch piece of black foam core or mat board

Black fat-tip marker (optional)

Clear-drying glue (optional)

Archival tape

Heavy black thread or lightweight black cord

The pictured 6-foot tree features 40 Printed and Hand-colored Planets and Stars.

1 Print templates on white archival inkjet paper. Or feel free to improvise, drawing and painting your own cosmos with a pencil and waterproof ink. Hand-color the art with watercolor and gouache. Allow to dry. Rough-cut around objects with scissors or a utility knife, leaving a ½-inch white border. Use archival glue or rubber cement, according to manufacturer's instructions, to glue art to the foam core. Carefully cut out shapes using a utility knife. Use a black fat-tip marker to blacken the edges if the foam core is white on the inside.

2 To hang, use a piece of archival tape to secure a loop of thread or cord to the back of the planet. Heavier, larger planets will need two pieces of tape to secure a length of thread or cord.

VARIATION: Embellish stars with rhinestones if desired. Affix using white glue.

MAKE

PRINTED & HAND-COLORED SUN

WHAT YOU'LL NEED

Sun template (download at artisanbooks.com/newxmastree)

Computer, printer, and printer paper or pencil and waterproof ink

One 8½-by-11-inch sheet of white archival paper in a smooth finish for inkjet printing

White 100 percent cotton rag paper for painting, 22-by-30-inch loose sheets or a 12-by-16-inch watercolor block (optional)

Watercolor set

Watercolor brushes

Gold size

3 to 5 sheets of gold leaf with paper slip-sheet backing

Burnishing tool or spoon

Soft wide brush for removing excess gold leaf

Clear-drying archival glue or rubber cement

One 20-by-30-inch piece of black foam core or mat board

Utility knife

Archival tape

Heavy black thread or lightweight black cord

1. Print the sun art on archival paper or draw your own sun with pencil and waterproof ink. Paint the sun in concentric brushstrokes of yellow watercolor paint, graduating to darker orange in the center. Paint over the perimeter in lighter orange. Paint the sun rays pale yellow with orange and gold accents. Paint around the sun in vibrant blue. Allow to dry.

2. Working in small areas, paint gold size in open concentric brushstrokes in the center of the sun. Let the size dry until it becomes tacky (follow manufacturer's directions for timing). Pick up a sheet of gold leaf with paper slip-sheet backing and press the leaf to the tacky surface. Firmly rub a burnishing tool or the back of a spoon over the entire slip-sheet. Slowly lift the slip-sheet from the surface, peeling it away from the gilded area. If you miss a spot, you can use the same sheet to reapply (any remaining gold will have stuck to the slip-sheet). Use a soft, wide brush to remove little bits of gold that cling to the edges of gilded areas.

3. Repeat the gilding process to further embellish the sun and rays. Allow to dry thoroughly. Use archival glue or rubber cement according to manufacturer's instructions to glue the sun to foam core or mat board. Carefully cut around the tips of the sun rays, allowing at least a ¼-inch border. To hang, use two pieces of archival tape and thread or cord to make a picture-style hanger. Hang the sun in the center of the tree near the top.

MAKE

COMETS & NEBULAE

WHAT YOU'LL NEED

White, ultramarine blue, yellow, burnt umber, and black gouache

Newsprint or scrap paper

Stiff-bristle spattering brush, stencil brush, or even an old toothbrush

Two 20-by-30-inch sheets of black heavy-weight archival paper

Round-tip watercolor brushes

Utility knife or scissors

Archival tape

Heavy black thread or lightweight black cord

Assorted rhinestones

Clear-drying glue

The pictured 6-foot tree features 6 Comets and 3 Nebulae.

COMETS

1. Create the star-splattered paper (see box, below). Load a round-tip brush with the thinned white gouache and draw the comet head on the star-splattered paper, pulling long strokes out to make the tail. Continue painting the tail in long strokes, fanning out from the comet head.

2. Use a utility knife or scissors to cut out the comet, leaving a wide border of night sky around it. Cut jagged edges at the end of the tail. To hang, use a piece of archival tape to secure a loop of thread or cord to the back of the comet.

STAR-SPLATTERED PAPER

1 With water, thin white gouache to the consistency of cream.

2 Practice your spattering technique on newspaper. Dip the tip of a stiff brush into the thinned paint, aim at the paper, and run your finger across the top of the bristles, drawing them toward your body. The size of the drops will vary according to how much paint you load on the brush and how briskly you stroke it. If the droplets are too transparent, add a little more gouache to the mixture.

3 Spatter the sheet of black archival paper with starry speckles in different sizes to create a night sky. Allow to dry.

NEBULAE

Look up wagon-wheel planetary nebulae to use as references for your ornaments. (I used the helix nebula in Aquarius and the ear nebula in Cygnus for mine.)

2 Paint the nebula in thinned white gouache on the star-splattered paper, then add touches of color as you like. Glue a few rhinestones in different sizes for added sparkle.

3 Cut the nebulae into spiral shapes.

4 To hang, use a piece of archival tape to secure a loop of thread or cord to the back of each nebula.

MAKE

COLLAGED JUPITER & URANUS

WHAT YOU'LL NEED

Two 9-by-11-inch sheets of marbleized paper (select paper with patterns that flow in drifts and mimic bands of gasses on planets)

Scissors

One 20-by-30-inch piece of black foam core or mat board

Clear- and slow-drying glue

Circle cutter (optional)

Utility knife

Watercolor set or gouache paint in assorted colors (optional)

Watercolor brushes (optional)

Transfer paper

Archival tape

Heavy black thread or lightweight black cord

FOR URANUS:

Red rice paper or other red paper

JUPITER

1 Glue marbleized paper to black foam core and allow to dry.

2 Use an 8-inch circle cutter or a utility knife to carefully cut out the planet.

3 You can paint bands of gasses and "eyes" to add interest, if you choose.

4 To hang, use a piece of archival tape to secure a loop of thread or cord to the back of the planet.

URANUS

1 Cut a 6-inch circle from marbleized paper. Paint gas rings if desired.

2 Sketch a ring to encircle the planet on red paper. You can sketch a template on another piece of paper if you're concerned about getting it just right. Carefully cut out the ring or template with a utility knife. Slip the planet under the ring (template) to position. Use the transfer paper to copy your ring design onto the red paper; cut out the ring and glue it in place.

3 Glue the planet and ring onto black foam core. Allow to dry. Cut the planet and ring out with the utility knife.

4 To hang, use a piece of archival tape to secure a loop of thread or cord to the back of the planet.

1 Begin the garland in the back of the tree, on the upper left side. Drape across the front of the tree, on the diagonal, to the middle of the right side. Make a U turn and drape on the descending diagonal across the tree, ending in the back. Hide the cord behind the tree and plug in the lights. Adjust the layers of draping on the tree.

2 You can tuck nebulae or stars between the outer layer of tulle and the sewn tube if you like.

3 Hang comets or other celestial bodies in front of the Milky Way. Comets should hang on the diagonal.

4 Hang the sun in the center of the top third section of the tree. Dangle stars on branch tips and all over the tree. Position the planets and other celestial objects in your galaxy in orbit around the sun, smaller planets on the upper portion and larger planets below.

5 Select a star to hang on the very top if you don't have a vintage star topper like mine.

SHIMMERING
TINSEL TREE

Tall and slim like a flapper in an Art Deco dress ready to shimmy on the
dance floor, this glamorous tree is clad in a waterfall of dripping silver.
You must use real Lametta lead tinsel from Germany to create the look
of shimmering icicles. Mylar just won't do; it's too flyaway and lacks the
weight to hang straight. This is the magnificent tree my friend Sara Kozel
creates every year, a tradition she learned from her father.

TREE

White spruce, or any tree that is tall and slim with open branches

VESSEL

Stand with vintage hand-painted burlap tree skirt

LIGHTS

Small multicolored bulbs, wound in and out onto the branch tips

TOPPER

Sparkle Starburst (page 212)

COLLECT
BLOWN-GLASS
ORNAMENTS

COLLECT
SMALL
MULTICOLORED
INCANDESCENT
LIGHTS

COLLECT
LAMETTA TINSEL

COLLECT

21-inch-long Lametta German tinsel (available online), enough for a slim 6-foot tree

Contemporary blown-glass ornaments from Germany, the Czech Republic, and other European sources, including snow-covered cottages, clip-on birds, pinecones, musical instruments, beaded stars, teardrops, and spheres

NOTE: *Lametta* simply means "tinsel" in Italian, and is readily available in Europe. Because it is made of lead, it is not pet- or child-safe—so don't let anyone eat it!

MAKE

SPARKLE STARBURST TOPPER

WHAT YOU'LL NEED

5 heavy 12-inch-long bamboo skewers

55 to 65 thin 10-inch-long bamboo skewers

Utility knife

2-inch Styrofoam ball

19-gauge aluminum wire

Dowel or wood-spoon handle

Wire snips

Silver metallic spray paint

Newspaper

Silver glitter

White paper

Trim five 12-inch skewers to 8 inches, trim thirty-five to forty 10-inch skewers to 6 inches, and trim twenty to twenty-five 10-inch skewers to 4 inches.

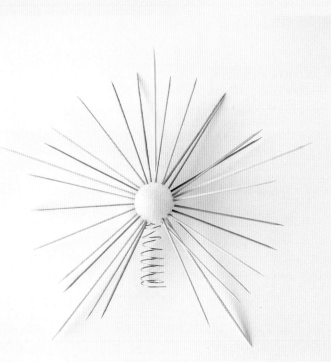

4 Insert the 6-inch skewers to fill in, on the same plane, around the five points of the star.

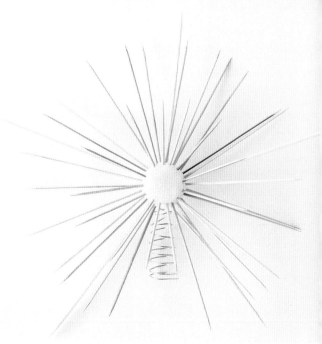

5 Insert a continuous circle of 4-inch skewers, positioning them in front of the longer skewers and in front of the wire spiral. Fill in remaining space using additional 6- and 4-inch skewers to form a flat-backed star.

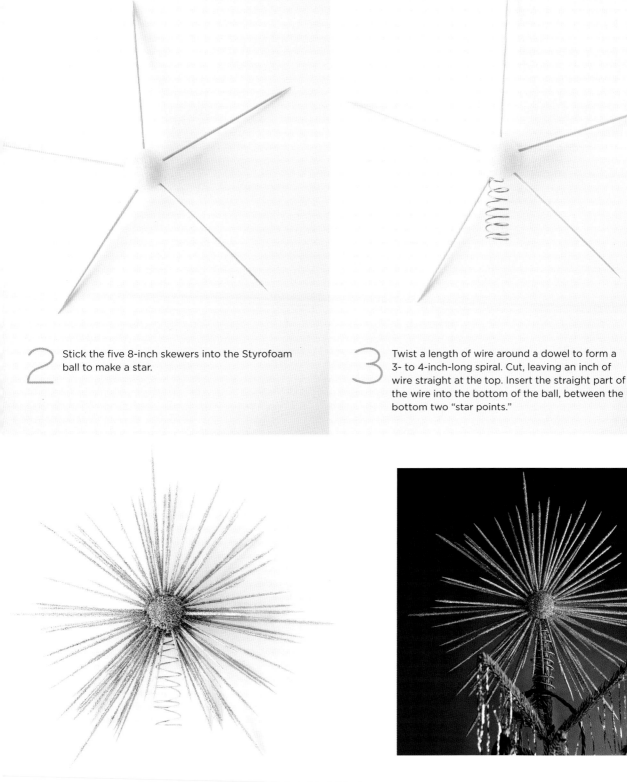

2 Stick the five 8-inch skewers into the Styrofoam ball to make a star.

3 Twist a length of wire around a dowel to form a 3- to 4-inch-long spiral. Cut, leaving an inch of wire straight at the top. Insert the straight part of the wire into the bottom of the ball, between the bottom two "star points."

6 Remove the wire spiral. Heavily spray-paint the entire starburst topper with metallic silver paint, working over clean newsprint, and apply glitter to the wet paint, working over the white paper so that you can pick up any excess glitter and reuse it. Allow to dry. Reinsert the wire spiral.

7 Slip the wire spiral over the top branch of the tree. Use little pieces of wire to secure it in place.

WHAT YOU'LL NEED

Five to six packages of 21-inch Lametta German tinsel

Several packages of white tissue paper

Facial tissues or paper napkins

Storage box

1 Once the lights have been strung and the tree has been decorated with blown-glass ornaments, open a package of tinsel. Carefully pick up a small amount with your dominant hand and drape it across your other hand. Apply *one strand at a time,* picking up each strand by an end and laying it on the tip of a branch between the needles, letting that end drape 1 to 1½ inches over the branch. The long portion of the strand should hang toward the front of the tree. Beginning at the top of the tree, continue to hang individual strands along the branch, spacing them about ½ inch apart.

2 Hang the tinsel on the branch tips and several inches into the center of the tree, creating a lush three-dimensional effect. Use shorter pieces of tinsel or a piece folded in half on branches where the vertical space between branches is too short to hang a full-length strand.

3 Every so often, take a look from a distance to check for even distribution of tinsel. Have patience: This process takes time. When you think you're done, go back and add a little more! This tree looks most dramatic with loads of shimmer.

TO REMOVE AND STORE TINSEL:

The beauty of investing in real tinsel is that if you store it properly, you can use it over and over again. Remove the tinsel the way you applied it, neatly and carefully! Pick up one piece at a time, drawing each strand gently through the needles and off the branch with one hand and draping it across the other hand. Lead tinsel is fragile, so don't tug.

 After you have collected a sizable hank of tinsel, lay it flat on several sheets of tissue paper and tie it with a piece of tissue or napkin.

Continue to collect all the tinsel and bundle the strands, placing them several inches apart on the tissue paper.

 Roll up the tissue and store the tinsel flat in a box for future use.

PIN TREE

Some collections start innocently enough with a handful of something; it's almost like the objects find you. Then the desire to acquire turns into a relentless pursuit. Friends join in the hunt, and before you can say "pincushion," you have enough tomatoes and strawberries to decorate a Christmas tree!

Serendipitously, as my collection of pincushions accumulated, I came across the exquisitely tactile bugle-bead-and-sequin-pinned balls made by Creative Growth artist Monica Valentine, who is blind. Her multicolored orbs inspired a re-creation, adding the perfect touch of sparkly pizzazz to this prickly-pinned tree.

TREE
White pine, or any tree with strong branches

VESSEL
Stand draped with natural-colored burlap

LIGHTS
White LED "seed" lights wound tightly inside the tree and out to midbranch

TOPPER
Tomato-Red Star (page 219)

UNDER THE TREE
Vintage felt letters embellished with sequins spelling "Christmas"

MAKE
SEQUIN & BUGLE
BEAD BALLS
(page 221)

COLLECT
VINTAGE FELT
LETTERS

MAKE
**TOMATO-RED
STAR TOPPER**
(page 222)

COLLECT
**VINTAGE
PINCUSHIONS**

COLLECT
**WHITE LED
"SEED" LIGHTS**

MAKE
**EMBELLISHED
PINCUSHIONS**
(page 220)

MAKE

EMBELLISHED PINCUSHIONS

WHAT YOU'LL NEED

New and vintage tomato and strawberry pincushions, in multiple sizes and fabrics

Narrow velvet ribbons, embroidery floss, thread, and trim in shades of green

Plain and decorative pins with multicolored and pearled heads

Needle (optional)

Thimble (optional)

Sequins

Bugle beads

The pictured 4-foot tree features 26 Embellished Pincushions.

 Pin or sew loops of ribbon to the top of the pincushion for hanging. A thimble is helpful to push needle and thread through the tops of stiff pincushions filled with densely packed fine sawdust.

2 To decorate: Add pins to the pincushion, randomly or in rows as you please; pin on sequins and bugle beads for extra embellishment.

MAKE

SEQUIN & BUGLE BEAD BALLS

WHAT YOU'LL NEED

Styrofoam balls in 1-inch, 1½-inch, 2-inch, 2½-inch, 3-inch, and 4-inch sizes

Long gold straight pins

Bugle beads in shades of gold or silver

Clear-drying glue

Sequins in a variety of colors; these are made with shades of pink, fuchsia, red, gold, silver, green, and turquoise

Delicate gold-wire ornament hangers and monofilament

The pictured 4-foot tree features 6 Sequin & Bugle Bead Balls.

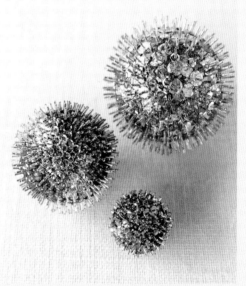

1 Decide what type of design you want to create: an allover mix of seemingly random colors or drifts of separate and blended colors. The objective is to create a pleasant modulation of color that changes as the ball is turned and examined on every side. Choose the size Styrofoam ball you want to pin. For the smaller 1-inch, 1½-inch, 2-inch, and 2½-inch balls, use one bugle bead per pin. For the larger 3-inch and 4-inch balls, use two bugle beads per pin. Apply a smooth coat of glue to a small portion of the ball before beginning to pin.

2 Thread the bugle bead(s) on the pin, followed by a sequin, and sink the pin as deep as it will go into the ball; the bugle bead(s) will act as a spacer stopped by the pinhead, and the sequin will sit on the surface. Continue sticking the threaded pins closely together until you've completely covered the Styrofoam.

3 To hang, carefully thread a wire hanger into the smaller-size balls and tie a length of monofilament around the larger-size balls and knot and loop around a tree branch, tying it in place once you have determined the perfect spot.

MAKE

TOMATO-RED STAR TOPPER

WHAT YOU'LL NEED

Tomato-Red Star templates (download at artisanbooks .com/newxmastree)

Computer, printer, and printer paper

Fabric shears

One 9-by-12-inch sheet of green felt

About ¼ yard of 36- or 45-inch-wide red lightweight woven-cotton fabric

Pinking shears

Needle and thread

Sewing machine (optional)

Polyester or cotton batting

Green embroidery floss

Gold and silver sequins

Red and green glass seed beads

Gold safety pins

Straight pins

Large sequins

1 Print and cut out the patterns (you can use your fabric shears) and pin to appropriate fabric. Be sure to fold the red fabric in half and pin through all the layers. Cut the red fabric with pinking shears and the green felt with fabric shears. You will have two large red star shapes, two small red star shapes, one large green top, and one small green top.

2 With the right sides of the fabric facing each other, topstitch the edges of the star shapes together, leaving one point of each star open. Turn the stars inside out, stuff them with batting, and hand-sew the open points closed. Wrap the green felt tops around the points you just sewed, and sew them in place. Using embroidery floss, attach the small star top to the large star top, leaving a length of floss in between so that the small star will dangle below.

3 Use the sequin-sewing technique (see page 290) to embellish the sides of the large star with sequins and seed beads. Use embroidery floss to wrap a star shape between the star points (like you're tying a package) on the front of the large star; tie a bow on the back to secure it in place. Decorate with gold safety pins and straight pins with large sequins. To hang, use embroidery floss to tie the large star to the top of the tree.

RAGGEDY TREE

Regally crowned with a gold ball of twine pierced with knitting needles and crochet hooks, this shaggy tree is a fashionable red riot of knotted, fringed strips of houndstooth, plaid, and tweed. It's an ode to Vivian Westwood, punk, and Cousin Itt, with a silhouette worthy of La Infanta Margarita Maria in a seventeenth-century painting by Velázquez. This anti-bow tree is ready to rock Christmas!

TREE
White spruce, or any full tree that is wide at the bottom

VESSEL
Bucket or tree stand (it won't be seen)

LIGHTS
Small white lights wound deep in the tree and out to the branch tips

TOPPER
Hook-and-Needle-Pierced Sphere (page 229)

TRIMMINGS

COLLECT
FLANNEL RAGS

COLLECT
COTTON PLAID RAGS

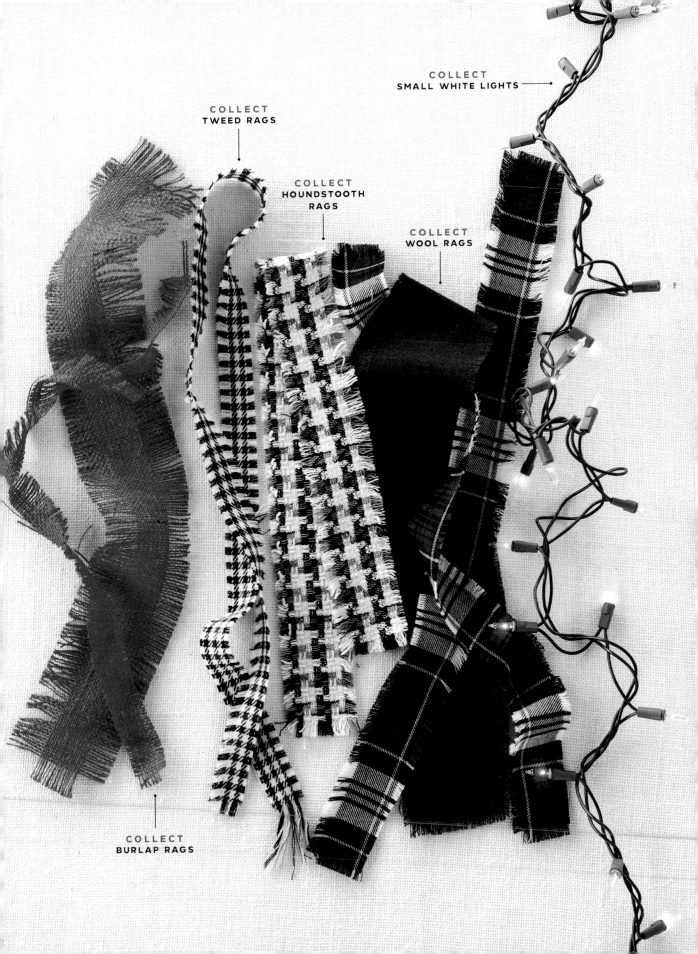

COLLECT
SMALL WHITE LIGHTS

COLLECT
TWEED RAGS

COLLECT
HOUNDSTOOTH
RAGS

COLLECT
WOOL RAGS

COLLECT
BURLAP RAGS

MAKE

RAGS

WHAT YOU'LL NEED

Woven fabrics suitable for fraying, including wool, flannel, and burlap

Fabric shears

Seam ripper

1 to 2 yards of 60-inch-wide solid red burlap

Large self-healing cutting board or large piece of mat board or cardboard

Straightedge

Rotary-blade scissors

The pictured 5-foot tree uses approximately 200 rags.

1   Use fabric shears and a seam ripper to deconstruct garments; lay out sections of woven fabrics and red burlap on the cutting board.

2   Use a straightedge and rotary blade scissors to cut sample strips from the fabrics. Use smaller strips (approximately 1 by 12 inches) for the top of the tree, midsize strips (approximately 1½ by 18 inches) for the center, and larger strips (approximately 2 by 24 inches, or longer) for the bottom of the tree. Tie sample strips on the tree with a simple knot in the middle of each strip to get a sense of your desired length.

3   Use your fingers to unravel the ends or sides of the strips to create fringe. Try ripping some of the lighter flannel fabric by hand to create a frayed edge. Start the cut with the scissors and then rip.

4   To create a layered look, knot strips on the tips of the branches and deeper into the tree. Disperse the different fabrics all over the tree, keeping an eye on balancing textures and patterns. Use the red burlap pieces to reinforce the predominance of red on the tree.

5   Let the long strips drape on the floor at the bottom of the tree. If you don't have enough long pieces, cheat the length by tying a knot at the end of a strip tucked behind another or under the strips hanging from above. Keep going until you achieve a densely layered look.

NOTE: Thrift stores are a great place to find fabric. Look for schoolgirl and adult wool plaid skirts, men's and women's flannel shirts and pajamas, and wool scarves and jackets.

MAKE

HOOK-AND-NEEDLE-PIERCED SPHERE TOPPER

WHAT YOU'LL NEED

4-inch Styrofoam ball

Jute twine

Scissors

Clear-drying glue

Metallic gold twine

Straight pin

Assorted knitting needles
and crochet hooks

Coiled aluminum armature wire

Wire snips

Hot glue gun and glue sticks

Floral wire

Wrap the jute around the Styrofoam ball until you have completely covered the ball. Tuck the end under itself and secure with a little white glue. Wrap gold twine around the ball in every direction, leaving plenty of jute exposed. Secure the end with white glue and a straight pin.

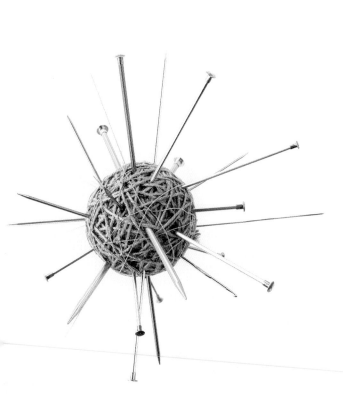

2 Pierce the ball with the knitting needles and crochet hooks in every direction. Leave space at the bottom for the wire stand.

3 Pull from the center of the coiled wire to make a cone-shaped spring. Gently twist the wire into the ball. Seal the wire to the ball with a little hot glue. Use floral wire to secure the base of the topper to the tree.

BEJEWELED TREE

This diminutive, ultrafeminine tree is an update on the costume-jewelry-encrusted ornaments and wall hangings from the 1950s—but less kitschy and more *Breakfast at Tiffany's*. Comb through your grandmother's jewelry box, thrift stores, and eBay for a sparkly collection of costume, vintage, and one-of-a-kind pins, earrings, pearls, and pendants. Permission granted to expand your treasured collection!

TREE

Small white spruce, or
any tree with small-
scale, sturdy branches

VESSEL

Antique bronze bucket
with watertight liner,
weighted with gravel
(see "Containers &
Tree Stands," page 14)

LIGHTS

Mini incandescent
white lights wound
deep in the tree

TOPPER

A large, dazzling piece
of jewelry

MAKE
VELVET & PEARL
RIBBON CANDY
(page 236)

MAKE
MINIATURE JEWELRY
FRAMES
(page 234)

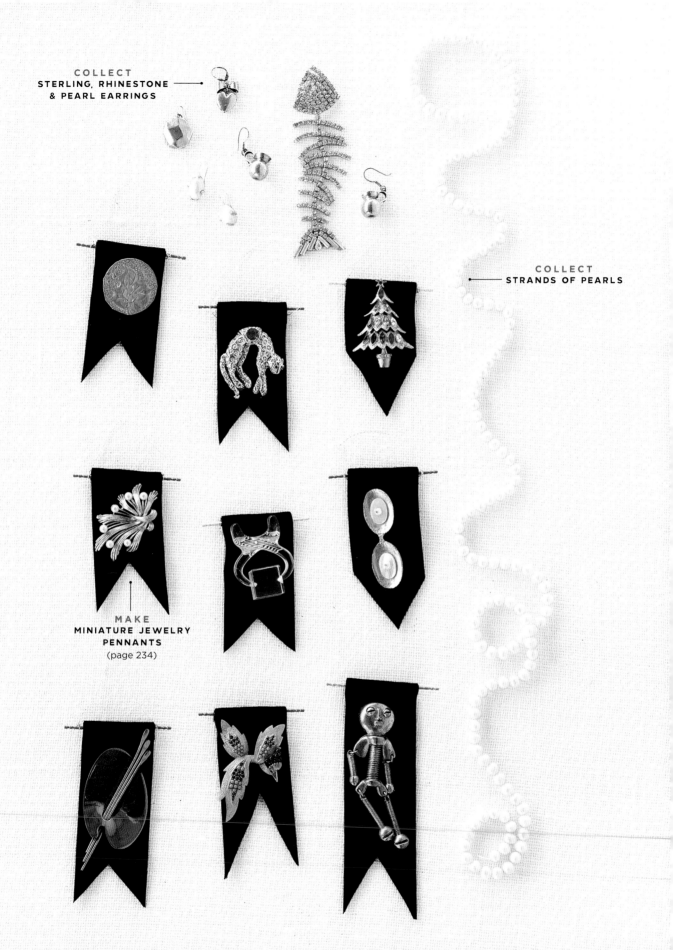

COLLECT
STERLING, RHINESTONE & PEARL EARRINGS

COLLECT
STRANDS OF PEARLS

MAKE
MINIATURE JEWELRY PENNANTS
(page 234)

MAKE

MINIATURE PENNANTS & JEWELRY FRAMES

WHAT YOU'LL NEED

Ornamental wood toothpicks with decorative ends (available at Asian or specialty markets)

Clear-drying wood glue

Pewter, silver, or gold metallic paint

Paintbrush

2-inch-wide black velvet ribbon

Hot glue gun and glue sticks

Scissors

Fine silver cord or embroidery floss

Needle and thread (optional)

Pins, earrings, or pendants

Plain round and flat toothpicks

Utility knife

Matches or a lighter

The pictured 2½-foot tree features 19 jewelry ornaments.

1 Glue two ornamental toothpicks together, staggered, decorative ends out. Make sure your ribbon is wide enough to cover the overlap; you want only the ends to show. Allow to dry, and paint the ends.

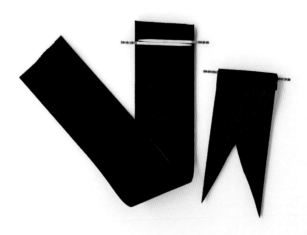

2 Select a length of velvet ribbon long enough to accommodate your choice of jewelry, allowing ¾ inch extra at the top and 2 inches extra for the tail. Fold the top of the ribbon over the toothpicks and hot-glue. Cut a notch or a V in the ribbon to finish the pennant.

3 To hang, attach silver cord or embroidery floss to the toothpick ends and tie them in the back. Pin or sew jewelry to the pennant and hang on the tree.

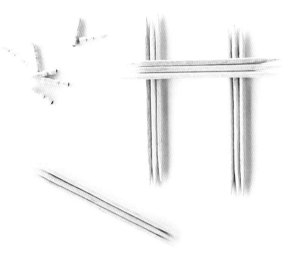

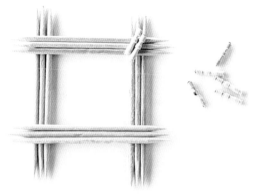

1 Gather twelve plain toothpicks and eight decorative toothpicks; cut off the decorative ends with a utility knife.

2 Lay out the plain toothpicks to make a frame, narrower than the width of the ribbon you're using for backing. Glue the toothpicks together with clear-drying glue. Glue the ends of two decorative toothpicks at an angle on each corner. Allow to dry.

3 Paint the frame and let it dry. Cut a piece of ribbon to fit the frame and singe the ends with a match to prevent fraying.

4 Hot-glue the ribbon to the back of the frame and let dry. Hot-glue a loop of silver cord or embroidery floss to the back of the frame. Pin or sew jewelry to the ribbon. (It's fine for the piece to extend slightly out of the frame.) Hang on the tree.

MAKE

VELVET & PEARL RIBBON CANDY

WHAT YOU'LL NEED

Velvet ribbon, ¾ inch wide
and 1 inch wide, in assorted
colors including black, purple,
midnight blue, teal or green,
and pale blue

Scissors

Matches or a lighter

Beading nylon or cotton thread
to match the velvet ribbons
(with needle attached)

Freshwater or faux pearls

Fine-point awl

Jewelry tweezers

The pictured 2½-foot tree
features 9 pieces of Velvet &
Pearl Ribbon Candy.

Cut the velvet ribbon into 6-inch lengths. Singe the ends with a match to prevent fraying. Make a long loop at the end of the nylon and tie a knot (this will be the hanger); trim the end. Thread a pearl. Fold the length of velvet ribbon a half inch from the end. Use the awl to punch a hole in the center through the two layers of ribbon, and thread the nylon through the hole.

2 Thread another pearl, fold the ribbon, and punch another hole. Continue to fold the velvet back and forth, threading a pearl between each fold to make ribbon candy.

3 Make a loose knot at the end, using jewelry tweezers to pass through the knot and hold the nylon in place against the bottom of the velvet. Holding the tweezers, pull the knot tight and the tweezers will position the knot snugly in place. Trim the nylon end neatly. You can vary the number of pearls and the width and length of ribbon for each ornament.

1 Pin or use a fine piece of wire or cord to attach the top jewel to the tree. Hang individual earrings on the top branches of the tree. Use a necklace as a garland at the top or separate strands of faux or freshwater pearls, as illustrated, to use for garlands—make sure the pearls are knotted between before you separate the strands!

2 Hang the larger pennants on the middle and lower portions of the tree.

3 Distribute ribbon candy throughout the tree.

4 Hang the framed jewelry and smaller pennants on the top two-thirds of the tree.

UPSIDE-DOWN TREE

Upended and suspended from the roof beams, a tree is transformed into a floating Christmas apparition, raining decorations. Evoking a giant ball of mistletoe, it also makes a dramatic and dazzling chandelier. The theme is borrowed from the Grimm brothers' folktale *Snow White and Rose Red*. Pomegranates and crafted snowballs represent the two iconic characters, and strands of jeweled cranberries suggest the treasure stolen by the ungrateful dwarf from the spellbound bear. The perennial twin morals of the story—*don't be deceived by appearance*s and *always do the kind thing*—seem apropos to the season.

TREE

Noble fir, short with
a 3- to 4-foot base,
or any tree with
strong branches

LIGHTS

Tiny white LED "seed"
lights, wound deep in
the tree and out to the
branch tips

SUSPENSION

2 to 3 yards of
natural rope and rope
pulley block-and-
tackle hoist system
with a hook attached

MAKE
YARN SNOWBALLS
(page 244)

MAKE
TULLE SNOWBALLS
(page 246)

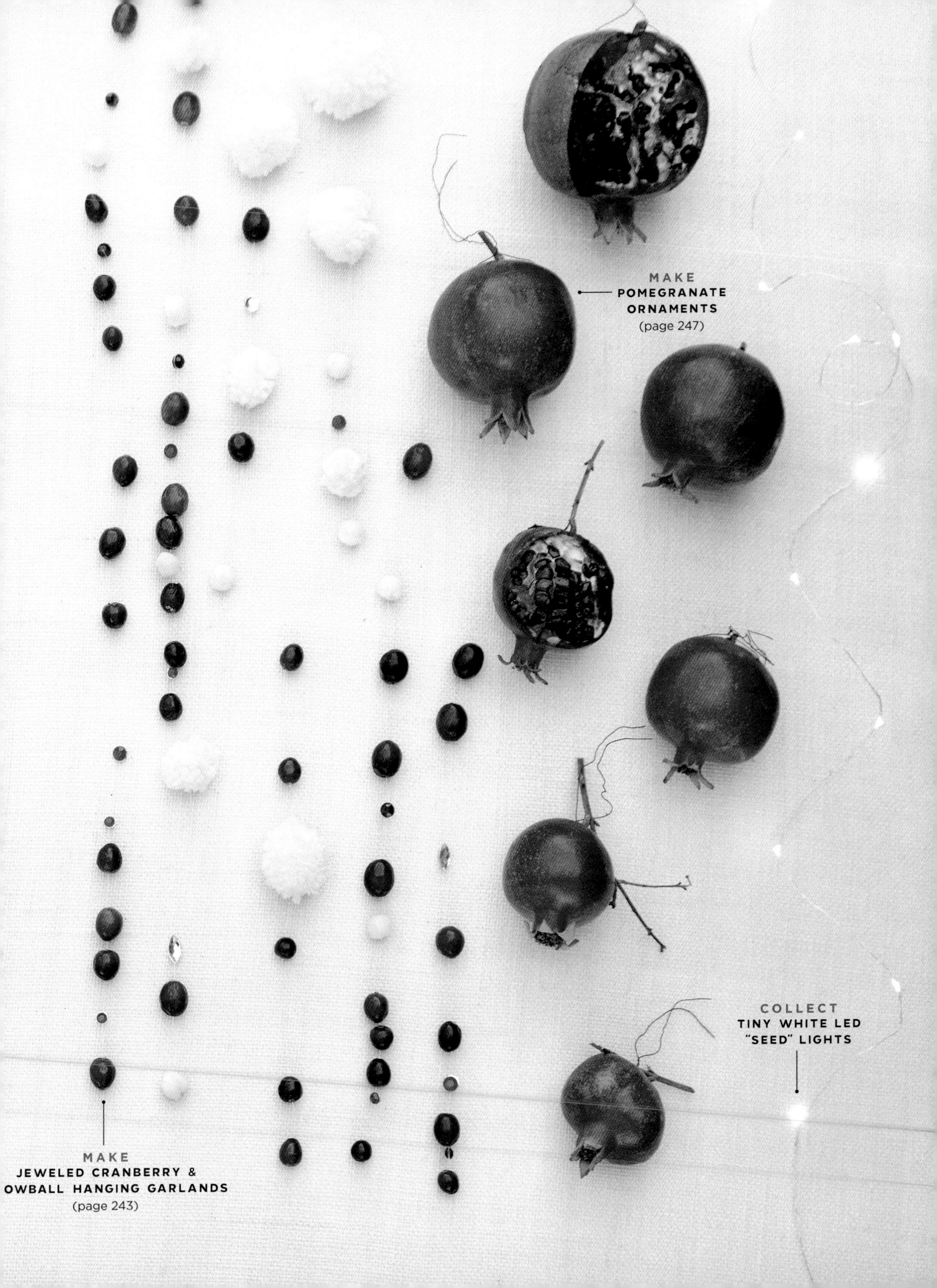

MAKE
**POMEGRANATE
ORNAMENTS**
(page 247)

COLLECT
**TINY WHITE LED
"SEED" LIGHTS**

MAKE
**JEWELED CRANBERRY &
OWBALL HANGING GARLANDS**
(page 243)

HANG

WHAT YOU'LL NEED

2 yards of ½-inch-diameter hemp rope, for tying on the tree, and yardage to suspend the tree from the ceiling (commensurate with the height of your ceiling)

Optional: Pulley block-and-tackle hoist system with a hook attached, a hook at the base of the roof beam, or an extra piece of rope looped around the beam

1. Cut a 1-yard piece of rope and make a loop at one end; take the loop and tie it in a simple knot. Leave an 8-inch tail and approximately 18 inches at the other end.

2. Take the long end of the rope with the loop and wrap it around the tree trunk three times; tie a square knot.

3. Tie a second 1-yard length of rope around the trunk, leaving a short tail end. Wrap the rope around and around the trunk, about 4 inches, covering the first rope. Tie a square knot in back. This is purely for decorative purposes.

4. Hang the loop on the hook at the base of the block and tackle. Pull the rope at the top of the block and tackle to raise and lower the tree as needed. If you choose not to use a block and tackle, take a long length of rope, throw it over the beam, and tie it to the loop at the base of the tree.

NOTE: You can throw a rope over a roof beam, tie it to the tree, and hoist the tree to the desired height. Or, use a block-and-tackle hoist system to raise the tree to the desired height. Hang the block and tackle on the roof beam with a rope or hook at the base of the beam. Either way, you will also need a spot or toggle to anchor the rope end. Try to devise a system that allows you to easily raise and lower the tree, as you need to turn the battery-powered lights on and off.

MAKE

JEWELED CRANBERRY & SNOWBALL HANGING GARLANDS

WHAT YOU'LL NEED

¼ yard of white ½-inch pom-pom trim

Scissors

Clear stretch elastic gossamer cord for jewelry making, or fine monofilament, 5-pound weight

Large sewing or embroidery needle

Cranberries (make sure they're fresh and firm)

Yarn Snowballs (page 244) in the following numbers and sizes: sixteen 1-inch, nine or ten 1½-inch, five or six 2-inch, and three or four 3-inch

Self-adhesive jewels: clear, red, and garnet in assorted sizes

The pictured 4-foot tree features 25 Jeweled Cranberry & Snowball Hanging Garlands.

1   Thread the needle with a 24-inch length of stretch cord and tie a knot at the end. Cut the little pom-poms off the trim.

2   Pierce a tiny pom-pom or cranberry and slide it to the knotted end.

3   Tie a knot a few inches from the first cranberry or pom-pom, wherever you want to position your next cranberry, to keep it in place. Little pom-poms don't need a knot to keep them in position; in fact, you may want to adjust their position after hanging. Alternate stringing pom-poms, cranberries, and snowballs somewhat randomly; vary the spacing and order for maximum visual interest.

4   To add jewels between the elements, position one upside down and stretch the cord across the center. Stick another matching jewel on top, pinching it in place with your fingers.

5   Make a series of garlands of various lengths, alternating placement of elements. Make a few hanging garlands with snowballs in graduated sizes or just one snowball. Tie the garlands onto the lower branches of the tree; keep adding garlands until satisfied with the raining effect.

MAKE

YARN SNOWBALLS

WHAT YOU'LL NEED

White yarns, 1 skein each, in assorted weights and textures including chenille, metallic white, acrylic, and wool-acrylic blend with net weights from 2½ to 5 ounces

Pom-pom makers (Clover brand) in the following sizes: ¾ inch to 1 inch extra-small; 2½-inch to 3⅜-inch large; and 4½-inch extra-large

Sharp scissors

Clear stretch elastic gossamer cord or fine monofilament

Large sewing or embroidery needle

The pictured 4-foot tree features six 5-inch, five 4-inch, seven 3½-inch, eight 2½-inch, eleven 1½-inch, and fifteen 1-inch Yarn Snowballs.

To make a 4-inch pom-pom, unhinge the arms of the 2½-inch pom-pom maker and begin to wrap the yarn around the arms.

 Tightly tie a string between the arms of the pom-pom maker and remove the pom-pom.

 Trim the pom-pom with sharp scissors to shape into a sphere.

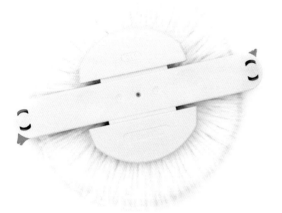

2   When you have completely and evenly wrapped both sides of the pom-pom maker, snip the ends of the yarn and close the arms. The more yarn you use, the denser and fuller your pom-pom will be. The pictured snowball was wrapped about 250 times for each side.

3   Snip all the layers of yarn on each side of the pom-pom maker.

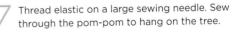

6   Make graduated-size snowballs using different-size pom-pom makers, or using different weights and textures of yarn.

7   Thread elastic on a large sewing needle. Sew through the pom-pom to hang on the tree.

MAKE

TULLE SNOWBALLS

WHAT YOU'LL NEED

Snowball template (download at artisanbooks.com/newxmastree)

Computer, printer, and printer paper

Pencil

Utility knife

Mat board

1 roll of 6-inch-wide white tulle

Small sharp scissors

White heavy-duty string or twine

The pictured 4-foot tree features four 3½-inch Tulle Snowballs.

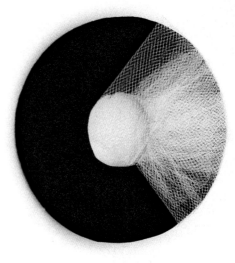

Print the template and cut it out with a utility knife. Trace onto mat board to make two 3-inch circles with 1-inch holes in the centers. Stack the circle templates. Cut five 2½-foot lengths of tulle. Begin to wrap around the circle templates.

2 Continue wrapping each section of tulle, completely and evenly covering the templates.

3 Carefully snip along the outer edge of the templates until you have cut through all the layers of tulle. Slide a length of string or twine between the two templates and tie it tightly. Remove the templates from the tulle snowball. Trim the surface with sharp scissors into a neat sphere.

MAKE

POMEGRANATE ORNAMENTS

WHAT YOU'LL NEED

Fresh pomegranates, in various sizes

4-inch nail or metal skewer

Pliers (optional)

22-gauge green floral wire

Utility knife

The pictured 4-foot tree features 16 whole and open Pomegranate Ornaments in assorted sizes.

NOTE: Work on cardboard or lots of newspaper; pomegranates are very juicy and will stain surfaces and your clothes.

1 Pierce the pomegranate with the nail or skewer horizontally through the stem end. It's fine if the piercing isn't perfectly level. Pull out the piercing implement; you may need to use pliers.

2 Thread an 8- to 12-inch length of green floral wire through the hole to wire the ornament onto the tree. If the pomegranate bleeds juice, simply blot it with a paper towel and it will eventually stop. To hang, wire some of the pomegranates on top of the branches and some from underneath.

3 To create the open pomegranate ornaments, use a sharp utility knife to cut away a portion of pomegranate skin to expose the seeds. To hang, pierce the pomegranate as directed in steps 1 and 2 and hang in the same manner.

 Once you have suspended your tree upside down, string the lights starting at the top, and hide the battery pack in the back. Tie large snowballs and wire large pomegranates snugly on top of the *upper* (formerly lower) branches of the tree. Add a few cracked-open pomegranates in strategic positions where the lights can illuminate the jewel-like seeds.

 Graduate from larger to smaller sizes of snowballs and pomegranates as you decorate lower on the tree. Tie some of the ornaments under the branches; it's fine if some are partially hidden.

 Tie the hanging garlands on the middle to lower branches to loosely conform to the tapered outline of the tree. The garlands may be somewhat random in length; this adds to the overall loose appeal of the tree design.

Once you're satisfied with the placement of decorations, raise the tree into position and secure in place.

TAPESTRY TREE

Velvet ribbon and delicate glass ornaments transform chicken wire and metal strapping tape into a pretty but slightly industrial two-dimensional tree. Use a sophisticated color palette of black, midnight or turquoise blue, emerald green, wine, and fuchsia with mossy and yellow greens and wintery pale grays for a rich, nontraditional Christmas tapestry.

Hang it on a wall if space is at a premium or, better yet, on a door so the bells can make a jingly, sweet sound every time it opens. It *is* a wonderful life!

COLLECT
JEWEL-TONE
VELVET RIBBONS

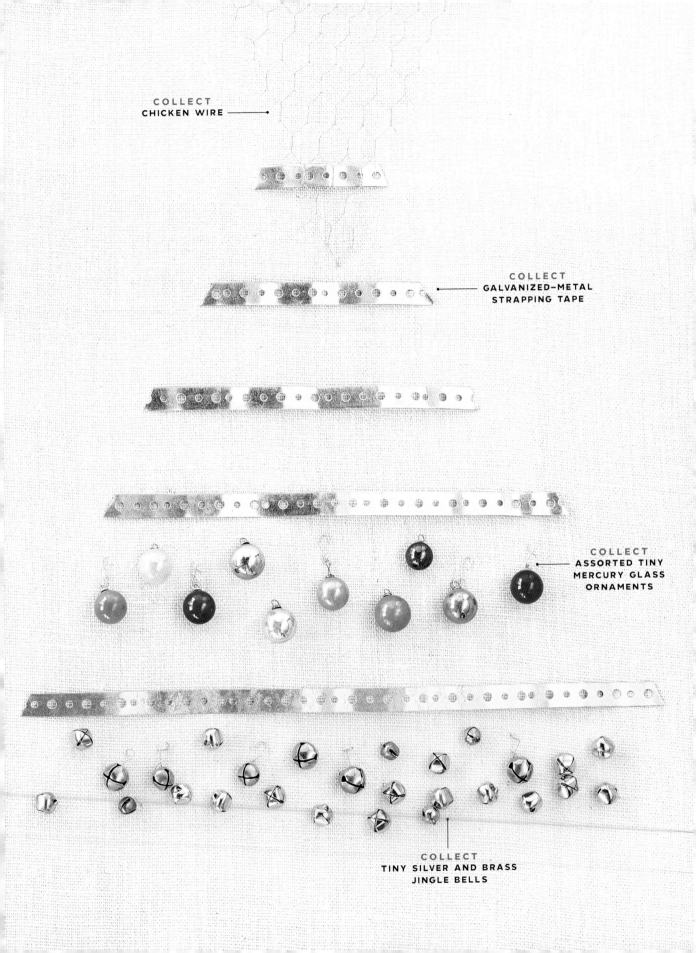

COLLECT
CHICKEN WIRE

COLLECT
GALVANIZED-METAL
STRAPPING TAPE

COLLECT
ASSORTED TINY
MERCURY GLASS
ORNAMENTS

COLLECT
TINY SILVER AND BRASS
JINGLE BELLS

TAPESTRY TREE

WHAT YOU'LL NEED

One 24-by-36-inch piece of 1-inch-mesh galvanized chicken wire

Straightedge

Color marker pen

Heavy-duty offset-handle wire cutters

Gloves (optional)

Roll of galvanized metal strapping tape

Assorted colors of ½-inch-wide, ¾-inch-wide, and 1-inch-wide grosgrain and velvet ribbon and velvet rickrack (1 to 2 yards of each of seven to eight colors)

Scissors

Sewing needle

Thread in colors that coordinate with the ribbon

Silver 22-gauge galvanized wire

Silver and brass tiny jingle bells

Silver ornament hangers or silver 20-gauge wire

Assorted tiny mercury glass ornaments

1. Flatten the chicken wire by weighting it overnight with a piece of cardboard and heavy objects like books, to facilitate cutting. Use a straightedge and a colored marker to draw a triangular tree shape, 24 inches wide at the bottom. Trace the lines several times so that you can clearly see the markings on the wire. Cut the wire carefully with heavy-duty wire cutters. (You may want to wear gloves to protect your hands when cutting the wire.) Follow the marked lines to the best of your ability. It's fine if the edges are a little wavy. Cut the bottom of the wire triangle through the middle of the last hexagonal row in order to leave a fringe of wire points.

2. Weave strapping tape in and out of every second hexagon across the second-to-last row of wire. (Strapping tape is too stiff to weave in and out of every hexagon.) Cut the end of the tape with the wire cutters, leaving at least 1½ inches extending on either side. Repeat, weaving lengths of strapping tape at gradually diminishing intervals until you reach a few hexagonal rows below the top point of the tree. When you've finished weaving, trim the ends of the tape at an angle that follows the line of the triangle and extending 1 inch beyond the chicken wire.

3. Starting immediately above the bottom row of strapping tape, weave a length of 1-inch-wide ribbon in and out of every hexagonal opening. Trim the ends 1½ inches beyond the chicken wire on both sides. Continue to weave rows of different colored ribbon, skipping rows of chicken wire at various intervals to create a pleasing rhythm of color and texture.

4. When you're satisfied with the look, trim the ends of the ribbon in line with the strapping tape. Carefully sew the ribbon to the wire at the end of each row. The chicken-wire edges are sharp and will scratch your hands, so work carefully.

5. Make a ribbon bow; cut a separate loop and sew it to the middle for a neat appearance. Sew the bow to the top of the tree. Make a simple wire loop and attach it behind the bow to hang the tree.

6. Hang the bells across the bottom of the tree and randomly on the tapestry using purchased hooks or S-hooks made from 20-gauge wire (see page 287).

7. Hang a few little mercury glass ornaments and bells on the tapestry with your hangers.

DRIED FLOWER & WHEAT TREE TRIO

Tall cones make elegant tree shapes, perfectly ripe for decoration. Two Swedish objects inspired this trio: a nineteenth-century hand-tinted photo of a bride in a flower-bedecked headdress, and a staff I received as a gift long ago from my husband that was festooned with spirals of straw-flowers. These tabletop trees wed folk-art themes with a modern eye, embracing the charm of sweet colors and old-world patterns and materials.

TRIMMINGS

COLLECT
STRAWFLOWERS IN
ASSORTED COLORS

COLLECT
TALLOW
BERRIES

COLLECT
BLUE SALVIA

COLLECT
GLOBE AMARANTH

COLLECT
LARGE
STRAWFLOWERS

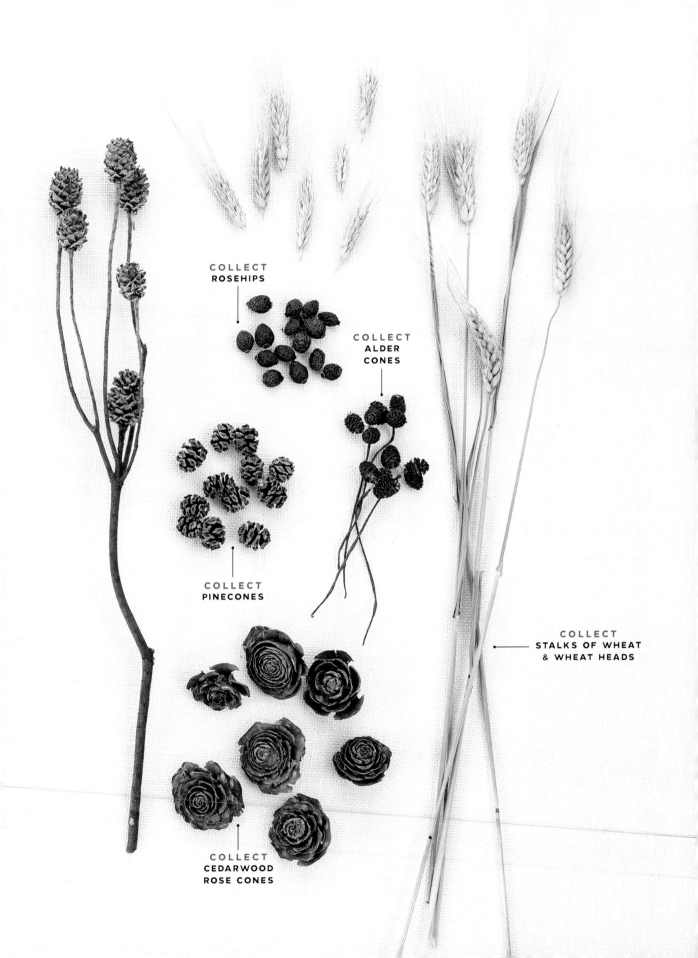

COLLECT
ROSEHIPS

COLLECT
ALDER
CONES

COLLECT
PINECONES

COLLECT
STALKS OF WHEAT
& WHEAT HEADS

COLLECT
CEDARWOOD
ROSE CONES

MAKE

DRIED FLOWER & WHEAT TREES

WHAT YOU'LL NEED

Dried flowers in assorted sizes, including strawflowers, feverfew, and globe amaranth

Tallow berries

Dried rosehips

Pinecones

Pint container or can

Styrofoam or pressed paper cones in three sizes: 14-inch, 16-inch, and 18-inch

Moss green and gold spray paint

Cotton string

Hot glue gun and glue sticks

Card stock

Wheat

Aluminum armature wire, ⅛ inch

Green jute

Scissors

Wire snips

NOTE: Instructions for making and attaching the jaunty feet follow the directions for all three tree designs.

TO BEGIN:

1. Organize the materials. Snip off flower heads from their stems; separate the different-colored flower heads, berries, and pinecones.

2. Use a pint container or can to help prop up each cone while you're working on it. Paint the flower tree cones green and the wheat tree cone gold in a well-ventilated area.

SPIRAL TREE

1 | Make a guideline for your spiral: Starting at the top, wrap a piece of string around the cone in a spiral, about two and a half times. Glue in place.

2 | Hot-glue a repeating pattern of flowers along the spiral string line. Continue to glue single rows or alternating patterns of flowers, pinecones, and berries, following the line from top to bottom. Snug the materials tightly together to hide the cone. Build adjacent rows with complementary patterns of contrasting colors, shapes, and textures.

3 | As you cover the cone with an ever-widening band of material, you will reach a point when you are no longer able to glue a continuous line from top to bottom, and you will be left with wedges of space at the bottom of the cone. Follow the spiral as best you can with shorter rows of materials to completely fill in.

4 | To create the crown topper, glue several bands of tiny flowers or berries, stacking one on top of the other, around the top of the cone. Glue upright stalks of wheat, salvia, and flowers on stems to fill in the top. Attach the feet as directed on page 264.

1 Begin by gluing a sprinkling of flowers and berries on one side of the cone. The richly textured, pointillist-style design of this tree is achieved by applying the smallest flowers and berries at the top, then gradually transitioning to larger flowers and pinecones toward the bottom.

2 Attach feet as directed on page 264. Fill in areas with variegated materials, alternating textures and colors. Use proportionately more of the natural and light colors, like pale green, blue, and yellow, and less red, hot pink, and burnt-orange, reserving those for accents.

3 Toward the middle and bottom of the cone, use clusters of little materials like tallow berries, filling in areas with drifts of salvia or other materials. Pull off the outer layers of cedarwood roses to use as leaf shapes, and glue flowers or pinecones on top.

4 To create the crown topper, make a small cone from a circle of card stock to fit the top of the tree. Glue on three or four alder or tiny cones, clusters of tallow berries, and a few tiny dried pink flowers; tuck in pieces of salvia. Glue the crown to the tree.

Glue stalks of wheat around the cone, heads extending beyond the bottom. Glue a second layer of wheat, heads only, above the first layer. Fill in the space between the stalks with more stalks.

2 Glue a band of blue salvia around the wheat heads. Prop the cone on a base. Create medallions of dried flowers and pinecones (see page 265 for examples). Play with different patterns and color combinations and build layers with extra materials to create relief and interest.

3 To decorate the top of the cone, cut off the wheat stalks evenly at the top with sharp shears. Glue several bands of flowers and pinecones around the top. Fill in gaps with tallow berries; place a flat strawflower on top. Attach the feet as directed on page 264.

4 To create the crown topper, make a small paper cone from card stock to fit the top of the tree. Glue five or six trimmed wheat heads upright, fill in with salvia, and add a circle of little flowers around the bottom. Top with tiny flowers and a strawflower. Glue the crown to the flat strawflower on the top of the tree.

TO CREATE THE JAUNTY FEET:

1 Cut three 9-inch, 11-inch, and 14-inch pieces of armature wire for the small, medium, and large trees, respectively. Straighten them as best you can. Fold about an inch of jute across the top of the wire and attach it with a bead of hot glue. Wrap the jute tightly around the top of the wire several times to secure, then wrap a single layer of jute around and around the length of the wire. Make sure you completely cover the wire.

2 When you get to the end, secure the jute with a bead of hot glue, wrap it several times around the glue, and cut the jute. Attach the end with another small bead of glue to finish.

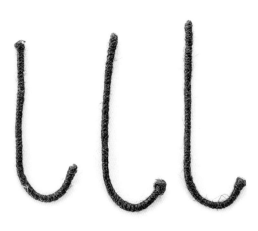

3 Bend each jute-wrapped wire into a J shape to make a foot.

4 Carefully poke the feet into the bottom of the cones, spacing them equally in a triangle. Adjust the feet and straighten the cones.

THE GIVING TREE

Reinvent the Advent calendar to make the holidays a season of giving instead of getting. Mark each day in December with your children as you count down to Christmas by opening a small envelope found on the tree. Each child selects one and follows the good-deed instructions inside. Make this tree on bare branches if you want to start the Advent countdown on December 1. Or choose a live tree and begin mid-month. Decorate the tree with an *abbondanza* of fruits and vegetables in overflowing baskets that reflect the theme of generosity.

a donation to a food bank.

Give someone a hug.

g it for your grandparents.

TREE
Bare madrone branch, or any other sturdy foraged branch

VESSEL
Old wooden grain bucket, weighted with gravel (see "Containers & Tree Stands," page 14)

LIGHTS
Tiny white LED "seed" lights wrapped around and between the branches

TRIMMINGS

Hold the door open for someone carrying packages.

Offer to do a chore you don't usually do.

Give a special treat to a neighbor.

Make a donation to a food bank.

Thank someone you see every day for doing their job.

Compliment someone you know is shy.

Make the bed for your sister.

Smile at someone who looks sad.

Offer to let another person go ahead of you in line.

Draw a flower or heart and leave it so someone can find it.

Give someone a hug.

MAKE
GOOD DEED SLIPS
(page 273)

MAKE
DECORATIVE
PAPER
ENVELOPES
(page 272)

COLLECT
FRUIT AND VEGETABLE
ORNAMENTS

COLLECT
TINY WHITE LED
"SEED" LIGHTS

COLLECT
FLOCKED FRUITS

COLLECT
PAPIER–MÂCHÉ
FRUIT

MAKE
WOOD-GRAIN
PAPER BASKETS
(page 274)

COLLECT

Fruit and vegetable ornaments, new or vintage in blown glass

Flocked fruit (Mine are from the 1970s; I added a little glitter to the leaves.)

Spun-cotton millinery trims and papier-mâché fruit in a variety of sizes

Baskets, including small wicker and woven reed. Attach ribbon, decorative braid, or cording to small baskets without handles; use hot glue or sew on with a needle and thread.

MAKE

DECORATIVE PAPER ENVELOPES

WHAT YOU'LL NEED

Envelope templates
(download at artisanbooks
.com/newxmastree)

**Computer, printer, and
printer paper**

Decorative papers

Pen or pencil

Utility knife or scissors

Clear-drying glue

Glitter

White paper

Cord or embroidery floss

Plain paper

The pictured 5-foot tree features
24 Decorative Paper Envelopes.

Print the template and cut it out. Trace it onto the back of decorative paper and cut it out. Fold in the sides, almost to the center.

2 Fold the top of the heart down to create the envelope bottom. Glue in place.

3 Fold the pointed end to create the envelope flap. Decorate with glue and glitter, working over clean white paper so that you can pick up any excess glitter and reuse it. Number as you choose. Tuck into a basket, or glue embroidery floss to the inside of the envelope at the crease of the flap and hang from a branch.

COIN ENVELOPES

1 Print the template and cut it out. Trace it onto the back of decorative paper and cut it out.

2 Fold in the sides and seal with glue. Fold up the bottom flap and glue.

3 Fold down the top to create an envelope flap. Decorate with glue and glitter, working over clean white paper so that you can pick up any excess glitter and reuse it. Number as you choose.

4 Tuck into a basket, or glue embroidery floss to the inside of the envelope at the crease of the flap and hang on a branch.

GOOD-DEED SLIPS

1 Once all the envelopes are numbered and decorated, fill them with good-deed slips. The slips pictured here were all typed on an old typewriter.

2 Cut strips with a paper cutter or scissors, write or type your message, and insert into envelopes.

Give someone a hug.

Make a donation to a food bank.

> **NOTE:** Examples of good deeds include: Smile at someone who looks sad. Give a special treat to a neighbor. Offer to help your grandparents with chores. Tell your family a joke.

MAKE

WOOD-GRAIN PAPER BASKETS

WHAT YOU'LL NEED

Wood-grain papers in contrasting brown and yellow tones

Scissors

Pencil

Ruler

Straightedge and utility knife

Clear-drying glue

Moss green or bright green crepe or tissue paper

Spun-cotton millinery trims

Papier-mâché and flocked fruit

Decorative Paper Envelopes (page 272)

The pictured 5-foot tree features 4 Wood-Grain Paper Baskets.

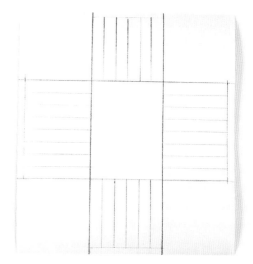

Cut a 9-by-10-inch piece of wood-grain paper. Position the paper wood-grain side down and make two vertical 10-inch lines, 3 inches from each edge of the paper. Mark two horizontal 9-inch lines, 3 inches from the top and 3 inches from the bottom of the paper. Divide the four rectangles adjacent to the center rectangle into ½-inch sections—six for the shorter sides, and eight for the longer sides. Make a ¼-inch perpendicular line along the edge of each basket side, creating a border.

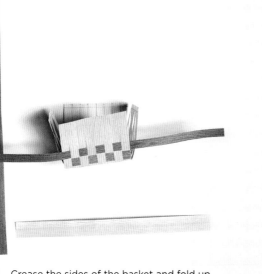

4 Crease the sides of the basket and fold up to shape. Beginning toward the center of the basket, one at a time, weave all four contrasting strips of paper in and out of the slits. Alternate rows of over and under strips. Crease the strips at the corners to make a crisp basket shape. Glue each strip to its end after weaving.

5 Fold the ¼-inch border over the top strip and glue in place. Add the handle and glue at the desired length.

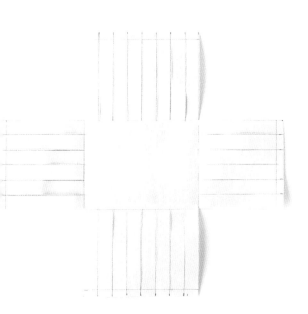

2 Using your cutting guidelines, cut off the four corner squares to create a cross shape. Use a straightedge and a utility knife to cut slits, following the guidelines from the center of the basket to your ¼-inch border.

3 Out of the contrasting wood-grain paper, cut four 15-by-½-inch strips for weaving. Cut a 1-by-10-inch strip of wood-grain paper for the handle. You may choose to use the same or contrasting wood-grain paper.

6 Shred or cut green crepe or tissue paper to make grass for each basket.

7 Fill with grass, fruit, and envelopes and hang on the tree.

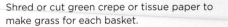

REFLECTOR TREE

Vintage and new reflectors glow on this brilliant tree inspired by decorations spotted on rural gates and alongside driveways at Christmastime. Collect reflectors in multiple colors, sizes, and interesting shapes—from truck stops, automobile-supply stores, and online dealers of antique and vintage car and motorcycle parts. Try to find a mix of tiny jewels that adorn license plates, vintage bicycle reflectors with sayings like SCHOOL'S OUT—WATCH OUT and DRIVE CAREFULLY, and marble-studded disks from old vehicles. Shine a light on this tree, and it will dazzle the beholder with reflected power.

TRIMMINGS

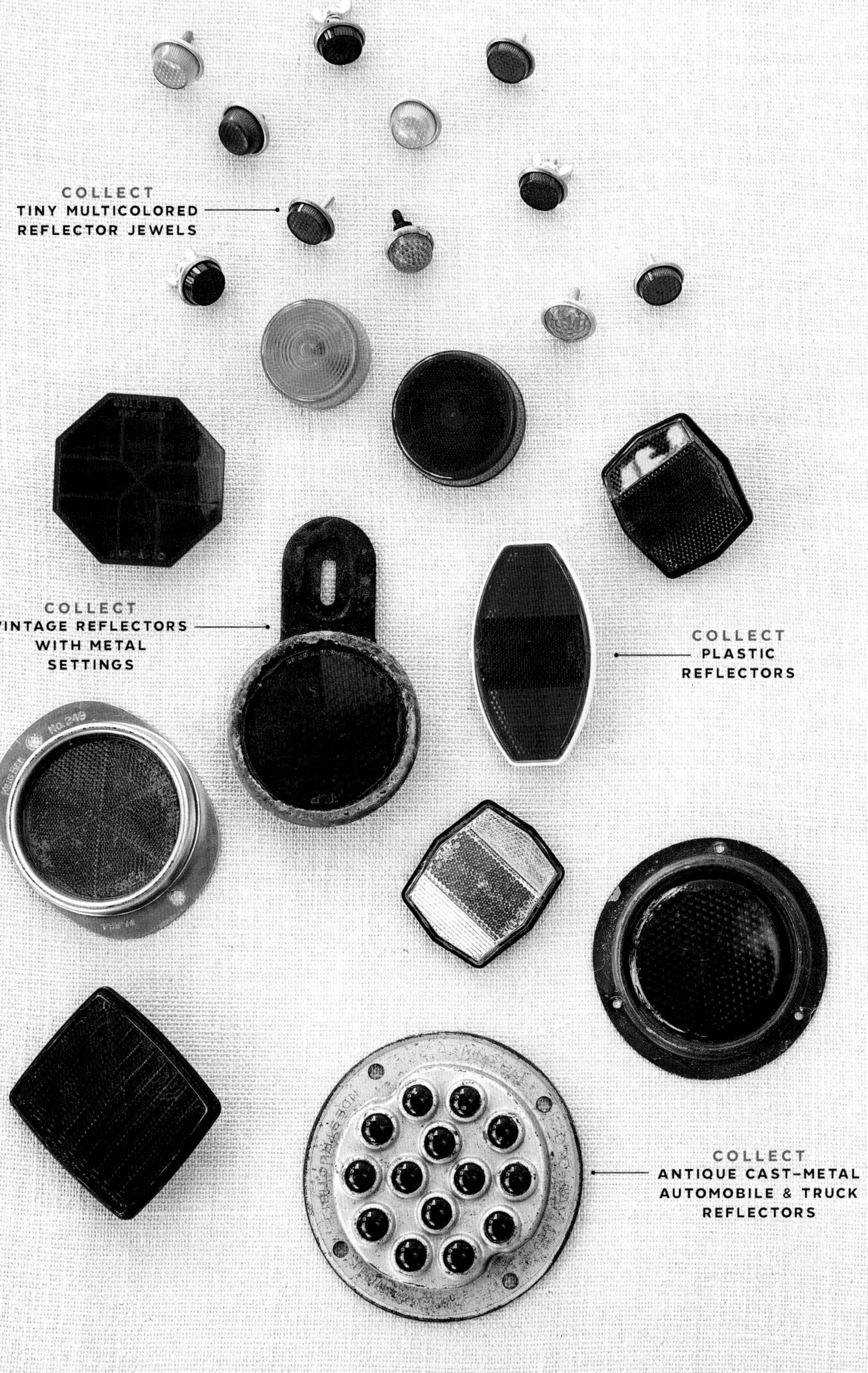
COLLECT TINY MULTICOLORED REFLECTOR JEWELS
COLLECT VINTAGE REFLECTORS WITH METAL SETTINGS
COLLECT PLASTIC REFLECTORS
COLLECT ANTIQUE CAST-METAL AUTOMOBILE & TRUCK REFLECTORS

SCHOOL'S OUT
WATCH OUT

SAFETY

COLLECT
LICENSE PLATE
DECORATION

COLLECT
VINTAGE BICYCLE
REFLECTORS

HELP
US
STAY
ALIVE

COLLECT
VINTAGE & ANTIQUE
REFLECTORS

MAKE

REFLECTOR TREE

WHAT YOU'LL NEED

¾- to 1-inch-thick pine
or plywood board,
at least 2 by 3 feet

Pencil

Hand saw or table saw

Waterproofing wood stain or
exterior paint (optional)

Brush (optional)

Assorted reflectors

Drill with assorted-size drill bits

Silicone or all-purpose adhesive

Assorted screws for
attaching reflectors

Straightedge

Screwdriver

TO HANG ON A WALL:

Two 1 ⅛-inch screw eyes

Steel picture wire
(15-pound or more)

20-pound capacity
picture hanger

TO STAND UPRIGHT:

2½-by-23-by-¾-inch-thick board

3-inch light T hinge (with three
holes on each side)

Six ½-inch wood screws

1　Measure a 2-by-3-foot-tall triangle on the board and cut out the tree. Seal the board with waterproofing stain if you are going to use the tree outside. Saturate the edges and back of the board following the product instructions. You could also paint the board with exterior paint. Allow to thoroughly dry.

2　Begin to organize the reflectors for your layout on top of the board. You'll want tiny ones at the top, graduating in size from medium to large at the bottom. Sprinkle some small reflectors in between the larger-size ones. Trace around the medium and large reflectors with a pencil, so that you can remove them one at a time and reattach in the proper position.

3　Begin by attaching some of the smaller reflectors with screw-back posts at the top of the tree. Press the end of the post onto the wood to leave an impression to show where to drill. Select a drill bit the same size as the post and drill a hole deep enough to sink the screw back in and mount the reflector flush with the board. Squeeze a small amount of silicone glue into the hole before mounting the reflector.

4　To mount the larger reflectors with screw holes, carefully use the drill to drive the screws in place. Flat-backed and pendant-shaped reflectors with one screw hole at the top should be glued in place to keep them from swinging. Apply a dollop of adhesive to the back of the reflector. Weight the reflector with a flat, heavy object while it dries.

5　Keep adding little reflectors in and around the larger ones until you're happy with the bejeweled look of the tree. If you have a special reflector like the safety star pictured on page 281, attach it on top.

6　*If you want to hang the tree on a wall:* Once all the reflector ornaments are dried in place, attach two sturdy eyehooks and string a length of picture wire on the back for hanging. Place the tree on padding when you turn it facedown to attach the hanger.

7　*To stand the tree upright:* Attach the long end of the T hinge to the end of the leg with wood screws. Measure and mark the center of the tree with a pencil, approximately 15 inches from the top. Turn the leg over and position in place. If you want the tree to stand more vertically, position the hinge lower on the back. Mark the three holes in the straight side of the hinge with a nail or an awl. Drill three holes with a drill bit slightly smaller than the screws. Don't drill too deep. Screw the leg in place with a drill or a screwdriver.

TOOLS & MATERIALS

CUTTING TOOLS

HEAVY-DUTY OFFSET-HANDLE METAL WIRE CUTTERS for cutting chicken wire and sheet metal. The offset helps to protect your hands from sharp metal edges and makes smooth, clean cuts. Use with gloves for extra protection.

JAPANESE FLORAL SNIPS for cutting twine, small branches, or fine-gauge wire. They're an alternative to a standard pair of scissors—something you probably already have in your toolbox.

PAPER SCISSORS for detailed, precise cutting of paper. Don't ever use them for cutting fabric, heavy card stock, or mat board—that will dull the scissors and possibly loosen the blades.

PINKING SHEARS for cutting zigzag edges; they're also useful for cutting fabric, paper, and even thin balsa wood.

A **RETRACTABLE BLADE KNIFE** as an alternative to a nonretractable utility knife; a good choice in the apron pocket.

A **RETRACTABLE BOX CUTTER** for cutting mat board and foam core (it's sturdier than a utility knife).

ROTARY BLADE SCISSORS for cutting multiple strips of fabric or paper with a straightedge and a marked self-healing cutting mat for accurate measurement. *Use with extreme caution and always be mindful of the hand that holds the straightedge; these blades are sharp!*

TITANIUM SCISSORS for cutting thin sheet metal; you can make precise curved or straight cuts.

UTILITY KNIVES (X-Acto knives) for all fine paperwork. Use both with a straightedge; practice cutting freehand shapes with the pointed blade. Change blades often when cutting lots of material—a sharp blade is absolutely necessary for clean precision cutting. Have a designated receptacle handy for the spent blades.

ADHESIVES

DOUBLE-STICK TAPE for mounting paper to foam core or paper to paper. The thick tape is available in several widths and thicknesses and is good for spacing elements slightly apart.

DUCO CEMENT (or other brands of multipurpose adhesive) for attaching metal to metal or to other surfaces, like wood or cork.

ELMER'S WHITE GLUE (or other nontoxic, washable brands, like school glue), a multipurpose adhesive, for a wide variety of projects and surfaces. It dries clear and strong.

FLORAL PUTTY—a green, waterproof adhesive—for sticking natural elements in place.

A **HOT GLUE GUN** for gluing a wide variety of materials and for a multitude of craft projects; the glue dries fast and clear. Use with caution—otherwise, you may severely burn yourself! Practice good technique by pressing the trigger and quickly releasing a bead of hot glue, pausing before you pull the gun away—this prevents annoying threads. You can also release a bead of glue and swirl the tip of the gun to wind the thread of glue into a neat bead.

NORI PASTE (or other brands of nontoxic, repositionable, water-soluble, acid-free, and slow-drying adhesive) for adhering paper.

RUBBER CEMENT, a slow-drying adhesive, for bonding paper to paper or to heavier board like foam core.

SPRAY GLUE for adhering glitter to a three-dimensional object.

WASHI TAPE, patterned Japanese tape that comes in a variety of designs and colors, for decorating paper projects.

WHITE FLORAL TAPE for wrapping white crepe-paper flowers and trailing vines or wire for paper projects. It pretty much sticks to itself.

WIRES, THREADS & TWINE

COPPER WIRE, heavy-weight 20-gauge for copper crafts projects and lightweight or fine 26-gauge for craft projects.

EMBROIDERY FLOSS for hanging ornaments.

GOLD ELASTIC LIGHTWEIGHT CORD for hanging objects and wrapping around beeswax ornaments.

100 PERCENT JUTE, available in different colors, for hanging ornaments and stringing pasta garlands.

PADDLE WIRE for wrapping greenery bundles and wiring floral elements to the tree.

SILVER ALUMINUM WIRE, heavy-duty 18- to 20-gauge for all manner of craft projects and lightweight 26-gauge for a variety of craft projects.

SILVER AND GOLD LIGHTWEIGHT CORD for hanging ornaments.

SILVER METALLIC THREAD for tying on ornaments or stringing lightweight garlands. (Metallic thread is also available in gold.)

WHITE FLORAL WIRE for wrapping white paper flowers.

HAMMERS, PLIERS, PUNCHES & MORE

BALL-PEEN HAMMER for hammering metal textures, especially for tin ornaments.

CLAW HAMMER, lightweight, for hammering nails and tacks and using nails to punch holes in materials.

LONG-NOSE PLIERS for bending wire.

METAL PUNCHES, set of three, for marking holes in wood, punching holes in tin, and drawing or scribing on metal.

PLIERS for bending heavy wire and working on craft projects.

ROUND-HOLE PUNCHES in two sizes (1⁄16 inch and 1⁄8 inch) for all types of craft projects and for punching holes for hanging objects.

ROUND-NOSE PLIERS for wrapping and shaping wire.

SCREWDRIVERS, Phillips-head and flat-head, for screwing in screws.

STANDARD-HOLE PUNCH, 1⁄4-inch size, for all kinds of craft projects.

THREAD CUTTERS for cutting and trimming thread and cord close to the knot.

TWEEZERS for knotting cord or thread in place.

WIRE SNIPS for cutting up to 20-gauge wire.

STRAIGHTEDGES & GUIDES

CIRCLE OR OVAL CUTTER for cutting paper rounds and ovals—or else practice with your sharp utility knife.

CIRCLE TEMPLATE useful for making circles for all kinds of projects.

PAPER CUTTER for quick cutting and breaking down larger sheets of paper.

SELF-HEALING CUTTING MAT, marked in increments of inches, for cutting all manner of materials.

STRAIGHTEDGE for all types of measuring and cutting tasks; you must have a good one with a clean edge.

T-SQUARE for measuring and making square, precise cuts.

GILDING MATERIALS

GOLD-COLORED METAL LEAF. Each leaf is on a piece of paper that makes it easy to pick up and apply. (Metal leaf is also available in silver and copper.)

SIZE for adhering metal leaf. Follow the manufacturer's direction to apply and then wait for the size to reach the desired tacky stage before adhering the leaf.

ROUND-TIP SMALL BRUSHES for painting size on the surface to be gilded. Use the size and shape of brush you need to precisely apply size.

SOFT, WIDE BRUSH for brushing off the excess leaf after you have applied and burnished it to the surface.

GLITTER & MICA FLAKES

DARK SILVER OR PEWTER-COLORED COMMERCIAL GLITTER, made from cut colored plastic, for decorating monofilament or the Sparkle Starburst Topper (page 212).

LARGE PARTICLE–SIZE SILVER COMMERCIAL GLITTER, for adding texture to paper crafts like the letters on the Typography Tree (page 184).

MEDIUM PARTICLE–SIZE SILVER GERMAN GLASS GLITTER, the luxury ingredient glitter, for all types of paper crafts.

NATURAL-COLOR MICA FLAKES, in different colors and particle sizes, for adding an old-world appeal.

SUPERFINE GLASS GLITTER—which is indeed tiny shards of glass—for decorating paper crafts like envelopes or cones.

SUPERFINE GOLD GERMAN GLASS GLITTER, an elegant choice for paper crafts or for dusting wet glue on the top of gold-painted walnuts.

CHRISTMAS TREE HANDLING & TRIMMING TOOLS

FOLDING SAWS, available in different blade lengths, for cutting trees and branches in the wild or cutting a tree stump after it has been out of water for more than a half hour.

LEATHER GLOVES for protecting your hands from sap and sharp needles, especially when you are cutting down a tree or trimming large branches.

PRUNING SHEARS for trimming unruly branches, shaping the tree, and pruning close to the trunk. They can also be useful when foraging for greenery and branches.

TECHNIQUES

MAKING YOUR OWN ORNAMENT HANGERS

1. Hold needle-nose pliers in your dominant hand and a length of wire in your other hand (20-gauge wire for lightweight objects; 18-gauge wire for heavy objects). Cut the wire accordingly to make a long (2- to 3-inch) or short (1-inch) hanger.

2. Bend the tip of the wire around your pliers to form a tight loop.

3. Bend the other end of wire around the pliers in the opposite direction to form an S shape. You can vary the size of the loops to suit whatever type of ornament you are hanging, as well as the size of the branch.

4. To firmly attach the S-hook to an object like a bell, slip one end of the wire through the object's opening and pinch it tightly in place with your pliers.

MAKING A KIRIGAMI FLOWER

1. Fold a 4-inch square of green rice paper in half horizontally.

2. Fold the bottom right corner up to the top center; crease and unfold.

3. Fold the top right corner to the bottom center; crease and unfold.

4. Fold the bottom left corner to meet the center of the X created by the two previous folds; crease the fold on the far left.

5. Fold the point touching the X to meet the left of the outer fold creased in step 4; crease the right edge of the fold.

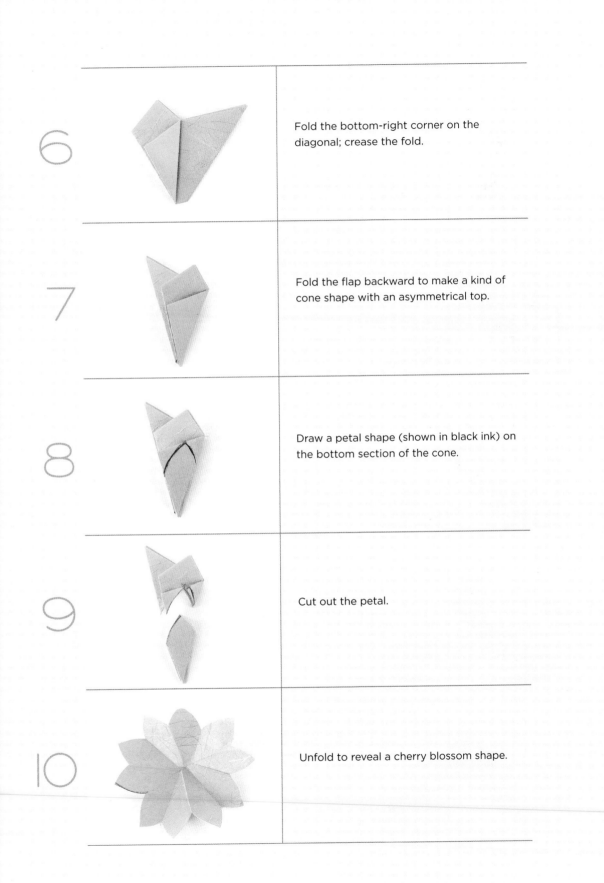

6 Fold the bottom-right corner on the diagonal; crease the fold.

7 Fold the flap backward to make a kind of cone shape with an asymmetrical top.

8 Draw a petal shape (shown in black ink) on the bottom section of the cone.

9 Cut out the petal.

10 Unfold to reveal a cherry blossom shape.

1. Thread a long, slim needle with your choice of thread and tie a knot at the end.

2. Pull the needle through the back of the fabric and thread a sequin and a seed bead on the needle.

3. Loop around the seed bead and pull the needle through the sequin hole.

4. Pull the thread tight, securing the bead in the center of the sequin.

5. Travel under the fabric and bring the needle up in the next spot you wish to attach a beaded sequin; continue embellishing in whatever pattern you choose. Vary the sequins and beads to your liking.

GINGERBREAD COOKIES

Makes 45 to 50 large cookies

3 cups all-purpose flour

¼ teaspoon sea salt

1 teaspoon baking soda

1 tablespoon ginger

1 teaspoon cinnamon

½ teaspoon freshly grated or ground nutmeg

½ teaspoon freshly ground pepper

¼ teaspoon allspice

Pinch of ground cloves

6 ounces unsalted butter, at room temperature

¾ cup firmly packed dark brown sugar

1 large egg, at room temperature

½ cup unsulfured molasses or sorghum

NOTE: If you are concerned with baking times, bake a trial cookie and let it cool to determine whether it is to your liking. I like them crispy as opposed to soft—all the better for hanging and decorating.

1. Sift the flour, sea salt, baking soda, ginger, cinnamon, nutmeg, pepper, allspice, and cloves together and set aside.

2. In a medium bowl with a handheld mixer or in the bowl of a stand mixer, beat the butter on medium-high speed until smooth and creamy, 1 to 2 minutes. Add the brown sugar and continue to beat on high for 1 to 2 minutes, until light and fluffy. Add the egg and blend on medium, scrape down the bowl with a rubber spatula, add the molasses, and continue to beat on medium speed for a minute until blended.

3. Sprinkle about one-third of the dry mixture into the bowl and beat on low speed until just blended, 30 seconds to 1 minute. Scrape down the bowl and continue to add the dry mixture in thirds, blending and scraping down the bowl after each addition.

4. Wrap the dough in a large piece of plastic film and flatten into a 1-inch-thick disk. Refrigerate for 2 hours, or overnight for best results.

5. Position the racks in the upper and lower thirds of the oven and preheat the oven to 350°F (300° for a convection oven). Line several ungreased baking pans with parchment paper.

6. Roll out the dough on a lightly floured board to ⅛-inch thickness. If necessary, sprinkle a small amount of additional flour on the board to keep the dough from sticking.

7. Cut with cookie cutters of your choice and transfer to the prepared pans, keeping the cutouts at least 1 inch apart. When using small cutters, you can usually lift the dough with the cutter and gently tap it to release it directly onto the pan. If you are cutting out larger shapes with a cutter or a sharp paring knife, use a spatula to transfer them to the pan.

8. Poke a hole at the top of each cookie with a bamboo skewer or a toothpick.

9. Bake small cookies for 7 to 10 minutes, checking them after 5 or 6 minutes to make sure they are cooking evenly and rotating the pans from top to bottom and from front to back. The cookies are done when firm to the touch, lightly browned, and very fragrant. Larger cookies will take anywhere from 10 to 13 minutes; check and rotate the pans halfway through baking.

10. Cool the cookies in the pan on a rack until set, 5 to 7 minutes. Transfer to racks to finish cooling. Store cookies in airtight containers until you are ready to decorate (for up to 3 weeks) or freeze (for up to 6 weeks) to use later.

ROLL-OUT SUGAR COOKIES

Makes 72 small round cookies (fewer if using large or decorative-shaped cutters)

4 cups sifted unbleached all-purpose flour

2 teaspoons baking powder

¼ teaspoon salt

½ teaspoon freshly grated nutmeg

½ pound (2 sticks) unsalted butter, at room temperature

1¼ cups sugar

2 large eggs, at room temperature

1 teaspoon vanilla extract

6 tablespoons milk

1. Sift together the flour, baking powder, salt, and nutmeg onto a piece of wax paper.

2. In a large bowl, using a handheld mixer, cream together the butter and sugar for several minutes until light and fluffy. Add the eggs and vanilla and beat for a minute until incorporated. Add the dry mixture in three additions alternately with the milk in two additions, beginning and ending with the dry mixture. Mix on low speed to just blend the ingredients after each addition. Divide the dough in half, shape each half into a ball, flatten the balls into disks, and wrap each disk tightly in plastic film. Refrigerate for at least a half hour or overnight.

3. Position the racks in the upper and lower thirds of the oven and preheat the oven to 400°F (350° for a convection oven). Line several baking pans with parchment paper.

4. Soften the chilled dough for a few minutes at room temperature. On a lightly floured work surface, roll one disk of dough out to about a ⅛-inch thickness. Using your choice of cutter, form as many cookies as possible, transferring them to the prepared baking pans as you go. Gather the scraps into a ball, reroll the dough, and cut out more cookies. Repeat with the remaining disk of dough.

5. Use a bamboo skewer or a toothpick to pierce holes at the tops of the cookies.

6. Bake, rotating the pans from top to bottom and from front to back halfway through the baking time, until the edges of the cookies are golden brown, about 8 minutes for small cookies, 10 to 12 minutes for larger cookies.

7. Remove the cookies from the pans and cool to room temperature on racks. Store the cookies in airtight containers at room temperature for up to 2 weeks or freeze for up to 1 month.

CHOCOLATE ROLL-OUT COOKIES

Makes 45 to 50 small cookies

½ pound of butter, cut into cubes (chilled for food processor method; at room temperature if using an electric mixer)

1 cup confectioners' sugar

1 teaspoon vanilla extract

Pinch of salt

2 cups all-purpose flour

½ cup unsweetened cocoa powder

1. Place all the ingredients in the bowl of a food processor fitted with a metal blade. Pulse until the ingredients come together and the mixture turns from a powdery to a dark chocolate color. If you are using a stand mixer or a handheld mixer, beat the butter in a bowl until creamy. Add the sugar, vanilla, and salt and beat on high speed to blend. Scrape down the bowl with a rubber spatula, add the flour and cocoa powder, and beat on low speed until incorporated.

2. With the spatula, scrape the dough from the bowl onto your board. If it isn't evenly dark brown in color, you can knead it a few times to make it consistent. Form the dough into a flat disk and wrap in plastic film. Refrigerate for several hours or overnight.

3. Position the racks in the upper and lower thirds of the oven and preheat the oven to 325°F (300° for a convection oven). Line several baking pans with parchment paper.

4. Remove the dough from the refrigerator and allow it to sit at room temperature until it gives slightly when you press it. Roll out the dough on a lightly floured board to about a ⅛-inch thickness.

5. Lightly dip the cutter of your choice in flour, shake off any excess, cut the cookies, and transfer them to the prepared baking pans. You can also slide a bench scraper under the cutout shapes and transfer a few at a time to the pans. Reroll the scraps; the dough is very forgiving. If it becomes too warm, press the scraps into a flat disk and refrigerate until firm but not rock-hard. The cookies can be placed fairly close together; they don't really spread when baking.

6. Poke a hole in the top of each cookie with a bamboo skewer or a toothpick.

7. Bake for about 8 minutes, then reverse the position of the pans from top to bottom and from front to back. Continue to bake until firm to the touch, another 8 to 12 minutes; the cookies should smell really chocolaty.

8. Let the cookies cool in the pan until set, 5 to 7 minutes, then transfer to a wire rack with a metal spatula. If you've baked the cookies on parchment, you can carefully slide the entire parchment sheet of cookies onto a wire rack to finish cooling. When cool, store flat in an airtight container until you are ready to decorate (for up to 2 weeks) or freeze (for up to 1 month) to use later.

ROYAL ICING

Makes approximately 3½ cups

3 egg whites

4 cups powdered sugar

SPECIAL EQUIPMENT
Pastry bags

Larger round or star tips

1. Place the egg whites and sugar in a very clean dry, deep mixing bowl.

2. Beat with a handheld mixer on low speed for a minute, until the sugar has completely dissolved in the egg whites. Beat at high speed for 5 to 7 minutes, until the whites become very glossy and stiff peaks form when you lift the beaters from the icing. Take care not to overbeat, and check your progress often if you haven't made this before. The peaks should droop ever so slightly.

3. Transfer the icing to a pastry bag fitted with the tip of your choice. You can put the entire bag in an airtight container; fold the tip upright or seal it with a piece of plastic wrap, and store it at room temperature for several days.

WHEAT PASTE

Makes approximately ⅔ cup

¼ cup wheat flour

1 tablespoon sugar

NOTE: Because it has no preservatives, the paste is perishable and will eventually sour and become moldy.

1. Place the wheat flour in a small bowl and add ¼ cup of cold water; stir vigorously to make a smooth paste.

2. Bring 1 cup of water to a boil in a saucepan set over medium heat, and slowly add the cold paste mixture. Bring the mixture to a boil, stirring constantly with a wooden spoon to prevent lumps until the paste thickens. Remove the pan from the stove and stir in the sugar. Let cool. Use the paste immediately or store it, covered, in the refrigerator for up to 4 days.

ACKNOWLEDGMENTS

Heartfelt thanks to my dedicated production crew of two—my dearest sister, Julie Brown, and adored associate, Haley Callahan—for your inspiration and moral support. Craft experts and true collaborators, you made my ideas even better than imagined. Special artistic credit to Julie for work on the Jewelry, Folk-Art, and Copper & Cork trees and to Haley for work on the Typography, Hansel & Gretel, Birdland, and Pin trees; in truth, every tree benefited from your collective thoughtful touch, skill, and attention to detail.

To talented photographer Paige Green for your discerning eye, flair for painting with light, good humor, encouragement, and patience; your gorgeous images make the trees come alive.

To my father, Charlie Brown, for lending his antique reflectors and patiently helping me construct the Reflector and Upside-Down trees. Thanks for tramping through the woods foraging trees, branches, and ferns and for a lifetime of arts and crafts projects/life lessons and loving support.

To Kitty Cowles, agent, advocate, and dearest friend, for sparking my creative fire! I'm so grateful you brought me this glorious project and helped me conceptualize a second book.

To Lia Ronnen, editor and publisher, for the brilliant idea and for allowing me to run wild with Christmas trees; your trust and guidance is deeply appreciated. To Bridget Heiking, tireless project editor, for patiently shaping, finessing, and thoughtfully listening. And to the rest of the team at Artisan, for helping me realize this beautiful book.

To my dear friends: Stephanie Chiacos, artist and seamstress extraordinaire, for your generous time in the studio and for nurturing me always. Sara Kozel, Shimmering Tinsel Tree queen, for your love of Christmas tradition and kindhearted sharing. Park Kerr, for lending me the perfect elfin tree stand and extensive collection of vintage toadstools for the Scandinavian Tree, and for always making me laugh till I cry. Mary Clare Anderka, for freely giving me hours of crafting assistance, encouragement, and goodwill. Lisa Palmer, for cheering me on in life and letting your little golden lights shine on my trees.

To Keith Garlock, second-generation Christmas Tree farmer in Sebastopol, California, for teaching me how to select, cut, and care for the perfect tree!

To Alexis Lipsitz, for polishing my prose and fixing all my participles: past, present, and dangling.

To Stasea Dohoney, blithe spirit designer and creator of the splendid topper pierced with crochet hooks and knitting needles for the Raggedy Tree.

To my Jimtown team, thanks for your support throughout the making of this book.

It was a privilege and pleasure to celebrate Christmas year-round with you all!

CARRIE BROWN is the owner of the acclaimed Jimtown Store in Sonoma County's Alexander Valley. She has celebrated every December for the past twenty-three years by decorating uncommon Christmas trees for the store, her home, and clients. She is the coauthor of *The Jimtown Store Cookbook* and frequently works as a stylist for books, print, and other media.